GREAT
UNSOLVED
CRIMES

GREAT UNSOLVED CRIMES

LOUIS SOLOMON

SCHOLASTIC BOOK SERVICES
New York Toronto London Auckland Sydney

Photo Credits: United Press International Photo: pp. 4, 102, 117; AP: pp. 9, 15, 17; Brown Brothers: pp. 21, 63, 67, 88, 124, 130, 135, 147; Wide World Photos: pp. 30, 36, 110; Bettmann Archive: p. 81.

Copyright © 1976 by Louis Solomon. All rights reserved. Published by Scholastic Book Services, a division of Scholastic Magazines, Inc.

12 11 10 9 8 7 6 5 4 3   6 7 8 9/7 0 1/8

Printed in the U.S.A.

CONTENTS

THE GREAT FREE FALL ROBBERY

Until the solitary passenger in the rear of Northwest Airlines, Flight 305, handed stewardess Florence Shaffner a note, the transcontinental journey had been entirely routine. The liner was on the last leg, Portland, Ore.-Seattle, Wash., of a five-stop run from Washington, D.C. What happened during that final hop made it a day to remember, not only for thirty-six passengers, and six crew members, but for scores of frustrated F.B.I. agents, an improvised army of sheriff's deputies, volunteer manhunters, hound dogs, and the regular U.S. Army and Air Force.

The author of the note, listed on the manifest as D.B. Cooper, free-fell into the heights of crime history as the only person ever to hijack a domestic airliner for profit without being caught or killed. Since that Thanksgiving eve, November 24, 1971, no other professional or amateur sky crook has successfully challenged his accomplishment.

Undoubtedly, D.B. had some special, technical credentials which helped him fulfill his mission. Just how expert he was about floating in air became a matter of debate. One thing that couldn't be argued was his ability to make himself invisible, a not inconsiderable asset for any criminal enterprise. Indeed, he left so few traces of his venture that even the fellow travelers on his trip to nowhere can be forgiven if they ever wondered whether he existed at all.

Of course, the record shows that there was a one-way passage bought by a man who gave his name as D.B. Cooper for the twenty-five-minute flight from Portland to Seattle. But there was no reason for the ticket seller to remember him. To aircraft personnel on the ground or aloft, all passengers tend to look alike, unless they're complainers, or Robert Redford, Joe Namath, or Henry Kissinger, or they don't observe the "No Smoking" and "Fasten Seat Belt" signs.

D.B. was not fussy, or demanding. He made no impression on flight attendant Shaffner and her teammate, Tina Mucklow, when they welcomed him aboard. Even after he completed his self-appointed round trip, the best that police prodding could produce from forty witnesses who had spent some three horrifying hours in his company was: "kind of swarthy," "sort of about fortyish," "about six feet tall." Somewhat more specific results of the police poll were that "he wore sunglasses," and a brown business suit. (The skyjacker's clothing turned out to be one of the most bewildering aspects of the caper.)

Oh, yes, add his carry-on luggage, the beat-up briefcase on his lap. It wasn't much help in identifying him, but without it, his note would have been ignored.

The fact that he had chosen to sit by himself way back in the tail was not noteworthy until after D.B. had made his move. Then it became apparent the seating arrangement was part of his plan. He was perched on the cat-bird seat. Like the outlaw in a western movie saloon, his back was to the wall, nobody could surprise him from behind, and he could keep a commanding eye on the happening.

Minutes after take-off, when passengers could smoke, D.B. made his debut. Flight attendant Shaffner responded to a push-button signal, ready for almost any kind of reasonable or unreasonable request for attention, including, she thought at first, this one.

Like most attractive hostesses, Ms. Shaffner was not unaccustomed to occasional maneuvers of machismo toward her. By training and experience she knew how to cool the passionate without causing hard feelings. Sunglasses' approach was different from the usual pass. Less robust. More self-effacing.

An artist's composite sketch of the man called D.B. Cooper.

He said nothing, just handed her a folded slip of paper.

Ms. Shaffner assumed her pen-pal was too shy to speak his declaration of affection out loud. Nevertheless, as she put it:

"I thought he was trying to hustle me."

Since the customer is always right, or almost always, she tried to evade the issue by not reading it on the spot. Her appreciative smile was designed to say she needed time to read and consider the proposal. However, the author's intentions were far less honorable than she had imagined.

"I stuffed the note in my pocket and he motioned I should take it out and read it."

His gestures were insistent and demanding. Well, if that would make him happy...

Passenger R. Simmons who happened to glance idly back toward the hostess while she read, recollected much later:

"I saw her face drop. She looked bewildered and gulped." But he minded his own business.

Although the note was short, succint, legible, and Ms. Shaffner is not a slow reader, it took her time to get the message.

It demanded 10,000 twenty-dollar bills and two sport parachutes or else Flight 305's passengers and crew would be blown up.

"Could this be for real?" she was asking herself when D.B. answered in dumb show. He snapped open his briefcase. In it were two menacing red cylinders attached to coils of wire.

It speaks well for Ms. Shaffner's grace under pressure that her only visible reaction was a gulp. It was a panicky time for plane people. There'd been an epidemic of skyjackings, and not long before an F.B.I. attempt to shoot out tires on a kidnapped aircraft had resulted in three deaths.

In this scary atmosphere, nobody, beginning with Ms. Shaffner and including the legion of others to be involved, ever dared to assume D.B. was bluffing. Nobody ever was to know whether the threatening cylinders were real or make-believe bombs. Nobody was prepared to risk forty-two lives, forty-three if you count Cooper, as well as several million dollars worth of three-engined Boeing 727.

So that when the terrified young woman made her way to the cockpit and gave Captain William Scott the man's written instructions, Scott immediately radioed Seattle control for his instructions. Control in turn communicated with police and F.B.I., and with Don Nyrop, President of Northwest, for their instructions.

Nyrop to Scott: "Do whatever he demands."

Control to Scott: "F.B.I. and police have advised no action be taken. Repeat. No action be taken."

Exactly what action Scott or any other member of the crew could have taken, nobody knows. If anybody had any rash impulse to become a hero, or heroine, the orders from authority stopped it.

So far as the passengers were concerned all systems were go as the plane continued on its scheduled course to Seattle. They were blissfully unaware of all the consternation on the ground. Even when Captain Scott's voice informed them that there would be some delay in landing because of minor mechanical difficulties, they accepted the white lie without question. The only ticket-holder who knew about the negotiations with the authorities was D.B., and he wasn't talking.

The plane continued to go round and round in the air as a flock of Northwest employees hunted through Seattle banks collecting the required 10,000 twenties. Others were going crazy trying to locate the two sets of sports parachutes the hijacker had demanded. All this took time, and D.B. would not allow the plane to land until everything was ready.

As the slow circling minutes turned to hours, tension began to mount among the passengers. Uneasiness grew into worry and burgeoned into fear that there was something seriously wrong with the plane, and that disaster lay ahead.

The only exception to the general nervousness was Cooper. One of his fellow travelers' contributions to the subsequent police investigation was:

"He seemed kind of relaxed."

Part of the reason for the postponed landing was that when Northwest was ready with the cash and parachutes provided by the Air Force, the hijacker rejected the latter. He repeated his original demand for sport, free-fall parachutes, the kind skydivers use to aim themselves at a target on the ground. This communication he dictated to Mucklow for delivery to Captain Scott.

Scott relayed the message. Then, during the time the sporting gear was being looked for, he reported:

Scott to Tower: "The guy is getting antsy."

Tower to Scott: "Impress on him we're not trying to stall."

Scott: "He's getting impatient. We're going to have to come up with them (the sport chutes) pretty quick."

By the time Seattle was able to comply and the aircraft began its descent to a far corner of the airport, the twenty-five-minute flight from Portland had taken more than three hours.

It was only after they had landed that the passengers discovered they were hostages with much worse things to worry about than plane failure. For the hostages and the hijacker alike, the moments after the plane taxied to a stop were the most dangerous thus far. No one could be sure what kind of reception the collective mind of the law had worked out for the 305. Was there some kind of trap being laid? Would some eager beaver call D.B.'s hand? Was there a platoon of

The hijacked 727 jetliner, waiting for refueling at the Seattle-Tacoma International Airport.

trigger-happy snipers ready to let loose a rifle-fire barrage?

At this stage, the passengers were rooting for the bomb carrier. They hoped that nobody would try to interfere with his nefarious scheme, lest they all go boom. Fortunately everything went smoothly, and rapidly. The only hitch was when a Federal Aviation Administration official appeared and attempted to show Cooper the error of his ways.

Cooper's response was antsy:

"Let's get this show on the road," he growled. Not a very original statement but enough to brush off the F.A.A. A brief glance into a laundry sack bulging with twenty-one pounds of twenty-dollar bills, and a more detailed inspection of the parachutes, satisfied him. With an urgent wave of his hand he dismissed the occupants of the plane except for flight attendant Mucklow and the crew of the cockpit.

Keeping their distance, the officers of the law stood helplessly by while the hostages scrambled off the plane and headed gratefully toward their Thanksgiving dinners. The door of the plane closed, the jets roared, and 305 climbed up in a curtain of exhaust that ended this act of the drama.

Until now, the police and Department of Justice operatives had followed D.B.'s instructions almost to the letter, no matter how reluctantly. But they had no intention of letting him get away with his loot. By previous arrangement, a posse of three Air Force jets took off in its contrails.

The first reports to Seattle from the air trackers were that 305 was headed due south. South lay Oregon, California, Mexico, and Latin America. Word was flashed to colleagues south to look for the fugitive flying machine. Within minutes, however, the jets radioed that the 305 had changed its mind. It was now veering westward.

In Seattle, the freed hostages were still not enjoying their turkey and stuffing. They were being subjected to a grilling by law officers, desperate to get some line on Cooper. They answered the investigators' questions as best they could, nowhere good enough to clue the police in. They had much more information to give in answer to the profoundly inane questions that TV reporters invariably ask survivors of any ordeal: "How did you feel when?...Were you scared when?...How scared were you?"...questions.

For practical purposes, the sum total of all the witnesses' testimony was they really saw no evil, heard no evil.

In Seattle, official skull sessions made sorties into D.B.'s brain, in search of his next gambit. Obviously he had to get off the plane somewhere. What wasn't so obvious was, where? They could deal with that one because 305 needed more than a mile-long strip to land on. And they could figure pretty closely, knowing how much gas the aircraft had left, which airports were landing possibilities.

The parachutes stimulated a lot of head scratching. Were they an attempt to mislead the law into thinking the hijacker was going to flee the liner in flight, or were they a for-real part of his game plan? Was he out of his mind? Hop out at night? In a business suit? Into the snowstorm that swirled over the thickly forested mountain wilderness to the south and west? Was he the kind of nut who wanted to leave his footprint in the sands of crime by going out in a blaze of suicidal glory? Or had he come to his senses and realized that he couldn't get away with his loot and chosen to end it all? Anyway, why two parachutes? Crazy, man, crazy, no matter what else.

Meanwhile, back in the plane, D.B. was dictating answers to some of their questions. Tina Mucklow wrote them down and transported them to Captain Scott. They ordered Scott to head for Mexico. Tina shuttled back from cockpit to tail with news that the plane lacked the fuel to make Mexico. D.B. accepted this news without protest. Another dictation to Mucklow to Scott revised the flight plan. Scott was to head south toward Portland and then west to Reno for refueling, maintain altitude below 10,000 feet, keep flaps down, cruise at 200 m.p.h.

This time D.B. escorted Mucklow down the length of empty plane, and locked her with the new course into the cockpit, ordering all concerned to stay put. This was to be the last anyone saw of him.

There was, however, another later sign of his existence. A red light flashed on the control panel. It signaled that the ship's rear boarding ramp was being unlatched. The time, Scott noted, was 7:50. At 8:10 a second light signaled a fully extended ramp. This was not the way the 305 was designed to fly and Scott was having his difficulties. For want of anything better to say he called back on the P.A. to his sole passenger:

"Anything we can do for you?"

There was no answer. The time was 8:10 and the plane was approaching the wild wooded slopes of the Cascade Mountains. This area in southern Washington, where Lake Merwin is formed by the Lewis River, is rugged backpack country. The closest sign of civilization is tiny Woodland, Washington, which is only a couple or so air minutes north of metropolitan Portland, where D.B. Cooper had bought his one way ticket that afternoon.

If D.B. had indeed jumped at 8:10, around Woodland, as the law was to assume, he had not only injured Northwest Airlines out of 200 thousand dollars, but added the insult of not paying for what was almost a round trip. At any rate the crew didn't come out of the cockpit until the plane landed at Reno, some hours later. The only evidence he had left of his pioneering effort was one set of parachutes. Sunglasses, brown suit, sack of twenties, briefcase, twin red cylinders, and man had vanished into the thin, black, snowy, 7 below zero air blowing at 200 miles an hour.

The population of Woodland soared astronomically as it became the headquarters for what was proclaimed in the nation's press and on TV screens as a four-state manhunt. From Woodland, organized official hunters, including a U.S. Army detachment from Fort Lewis, and unorganized, unofficial hunters, slogged through 250 square miles of snow-covered, primeval forested Cowlitz County. A pair of Army helicopters chopped through the air over the treetops in which a parachute must almost certainly have been snared.

In return for their strenuous efforts to enforce the law, the members of the posse got nothing but unappreciative protests from fur trappers, who complained that hordes of searchers were bad for their business. After a week, the search was called off, on account of weather. As Cowlitz County Undersheriff McDowell had theorized:

"We're either looking for a parachute or a hole in the ground." Clearly, either one or the other would become more readily visible when the winter was over. But many suns later, when the concealing snow was gone, neither parachute nor hole in the ground, nor any remnant of D.B.'s luggage, treasure, or D.B. himself became visible to the human eye.

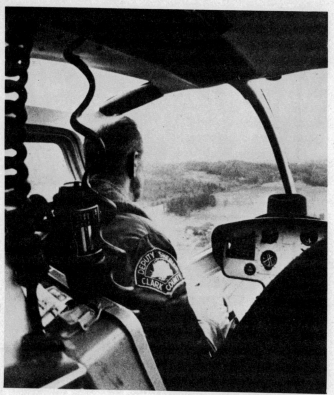

A helicopter searches in Woodland, Washington, for a trace of Cooper.

On the second anniversary of D.B.'s death-defying dive, Mr. Julius Mattson, head of the Portland office of the F.B.I., commemorated his agency's frustration with what can be interpreted as a tribute to the frustrator.

"We know nothing more about him today than we did on November 24, 1971."

So that while the file on Cooper is and will remain technically open, in the hope that some flaw will turn up in what has remained a perfect crime, it is, practically speaking, closed. This leaves the solution of the mystery to the deductions of amateurs. Their guess as to the possibilities and probabilities is at least as good as any of the failed professional thief catchers.

One supposition that can be eliminated from the start is that the police overlooked any clues to identifying D.B. Anyone who had had any glimpse of him looked vainly at mug shots. Fingerprints? There weren't any. Not even on the note he had written? Well, maybe there were latents on the note, and certainly a sample of his handwriting, but the police hadn't overlooked them. They were not available for microscopic analysis, because the hijacker had been careful to take his note back after it had been read.

Logic dictates that given the frightful conditions under which the leap was made, no parachutist had any chance to survive. In his brown suit, D.B. would have frozen to death before he landed. The fact, say some, that his

Newsmen interviewing (*from left to right*) Pilot William
Scott and Flight Attendants Tina Mucklow and Florence
Shaffner.

body wasn't found doesn't prove he isn't moldering away, or that someone hasn't found him, filled in the hole he made when he hit, and walked away with the money. Probable. Possible.

But suppose, just suppose there was a method to his mad bail out; the same attention to detail that every other stage of his modus operandi reveals. That method would have to posit that D.B. was an experienced skydiver — one of those daredevils who gets his kicks out of free falling to a target — who delayed getting his hands on the $200 thousand because he had to have the kind of jumping gear he was familiar with. And suppose further that this careful planner had prepared for his coup by practice jumping to a pre-set mark over the uninhabited terrain he disappeared into. And under the suit couldn't he have been wired against the cold? And who can say whether there wasn't a confederate waiting to ski, snowshoe, or snowmobile him away to safety? Improbable? Impossible? Well, maybe. But then, isn't the Cooper caper all of those things? Isn't that why it is the only one of its kind? If it weren't, the solution wouldn't still be up for grabs.

MURDER ON
FIFTH AVENUE

Even the most average, run-of-the-mill play-boy will make headlines when he's been murdered in his mansion, especially if he is sexily dressed for the occasion in black silk pajamas and is discovered by a genuine English butler.

When the victim who fitted these particulars happened to be someone as world infamous as Serge Rubinstein, the newspapers couldn't have asked for a more sensational story. The New York City police, who had to find the hands that took the mansion master's breath away permanently, were not so enthusiastic.

If, more than two decades later the strangler has not been turned up, it is not because the investigators didn't do everything humanly possible. Their problem was that before they could answer, "Who did it?" they had to figure out, "Which Serge Rubinstein was killed?"

This was infinitely more difficult than it sounds. Although there was never any doubt that the stubby (5′7″) body on the bedroom floor was the mortal remnant of *the* Serge Rubinstein — the same Serge whose rich, full, fraudulent forty-six years had been voluminously pictured and printed in the papers — still, in those forty-six years he had played many different parts.

When butler William Worthy's phone call brought the 67th Precinct cops to the marbled halls of 814 Fifth Avenue, on the morning of January 27, 1955, they didn't need a close of kin identification. The adhesive tape that sealed the victim's lips, the Venetian blind cords in which he was trussed, altered him somewhat, but it was Serge Rubinstein all right. And there on the wall was redundant confirmation — a blown-up photograph of Serge dressed for a costume ball, in the cocked hat and imperial uniform of Napoleon.

The tape and cords turned out to be useless as clues. And too many people had visited the third floor bedroom for fingerprints to be of any value. At this initial stage of the investigation the detectives paid little attention to the Napoleon blow-up, and ignored the statue of the Emperor prominent in the room. So he would have liked to be Napoleon. So what? So it told more about Serge, and what made

Serge Rubinstein in a happy moment.

him go, and what led him to his death, than all the subsequent investigation was to reveal.

Of course the Napoleon clue, if it can be called that, was only symbolic. Bonaparte was much more one-track minded. The power and glory he sought was in war. Serge was a man of many-sided interests. He was, among other things, a whiz-kid banker, a grown-up international financier, an ex-convict, a passionate collector of art, cover girls, Senators, Representatives, Ambassadors, politicians, socialites of high and low degree.

His versatility was known to the public and the police. Mostly because Serge assiduously advertised himself. None of his activities, however nefarious, ever resulted in a "no comment" to reporters. Unlike other glory seekers, Serge accentuated the negative — the amoral, dubious, and rascally aspects of his exploits. The tarnished self-image he helped create made him a top, continuing story in the papers. Of course he didn't tell it all. How much of what he told was true, or how much of it he believed himself, still remains to be seen.

According to his own account — the year he was killed he was trying to have his autobiography published — he had been forced, like his hero Napoleon, to retreat from Russia. Of course there were differences. Serge was ten years old, and he fled not the Czar's army, but the Bolsheviks. Unlike Napoleon he was an innocent target of Russian wrath. The Reds were after him because they disapproved of his father's job as consultant to the mad monk, Rasputin, adviser to the Czarina.

Clad in a size eight fur coat — he was small for his age — Serge took off over the iced Gulf of Finland in a three-horse troika, the Reds steaming on his trail. Sewn into the coat's lining was a Czar's ransom in rubies, diamonds, emeralds, and sapphires. And his underwear was embroidered with rubles and securities.

Several months later, the jeweled boy was joined by his parents and his big brother, Andre, in Stockholm. When he was about to turn fifteen, the Rubinsteins were living in Vienna, birthplace of psychoanalysis. Here he asked for a birthday present which would have confounded the parent of any adolescent.

The gift? Analysis by one of the founding fathers of that art, Dr. Alfred Adler.

Why not a bike, or an increased allowance, or a Rolls Royce?

"Because," Serge tells us, "I was afraid I was developing an inferiority complex."

Evidently his dad was convinced. But after only a couple or three sessions, Serge got off the couch for good. He remembers the experience vividly enough to quote Adler's parting words verbatim:

"If I cure you," the great healer said, "you'll be just ordinary. The way you are now, you'll be driven by ambition and desires."

Could even Dr. Adler have restored Serge to healthy ordinariness? Judging by the rest of his extraordinary career, it would have been a miracle. But if his ambition and desires had been sublimated he might have died of old age.

Thus far, nothing in his dossier was of any help to the police. Serge had not yet — as a teenager — succeeded in making any enemies except for the Bolsheviks. And they had dropped out of his life after losing the horse-race on ice.

By the time he was eighteen, Serge had made a modest beginning toward being cordially disliked. He was an honor student at Cambridge University in England. His big brother, Andre, advanced the money for his education. The relationship between the brothers was strained when Serge neglected to repay the loan. It broke not long after Serge came of age, when Andre sued to reclaim a couple of million dollars he charged Serge had stolen from him.

It was not until he was twenty-three that Serge made a major first stride toward collecting enemies — at least, the first giant step on record. This resulted from the birthday present he gave himself, $1,000,000. He was able to be so generous because despite his tender years he had become the hard-nosed manager of a Paris bank, Franco-Asiatique. Banking prodigy Rubinstein was thus in the right place — where the money was — at the right time — when a little inside information plus a lot of unscrupulousness could be converted into cash.

The bank was the financial agent for Chiang Kai-shek's China, which was a bad credit risk because it had defaulted on a bond issue floated through Franco-Asiatique. Undeterred by this disaster, China was trying to borrow money again with a new bond issue. But as boy-manager-negotiator, Serge pointed out that China could only help restore its credit rating if it paid the interest due on the new bonds.

The rest is banking history. Serge surreptitiously bought up the defaulted bonds for just a little more than their worth — nothing — and when China delivered the million dollar interest on the new bonds to Franco-Asiatique's manager, M. Rubinstein, he turned it over to the new owner of the old bonds.

As he proudly summed up the transaction:

"I had the bonds and I had the money. I just paid myself off."

Illegal? No. Unethical? Yes, by the rules of the banking community regarding employee conduct. But then, the investors who'd held the worthless paper could not have held either Franco-Asiatique or Serge or China in high ethical esteem.

The result of the slippery scheme was that Serge became celebrated as a financial whiz; and that the French government began a three-year effort to kick him out of the country.

Serge insisted that his ultimate expulsion from France was not really because of his double-dealing, but because he was irresistible to a certain titled lady.

"Pierre Laval (French Premier) was jealous of my *friendship* (italics by Serge) with his mistress, a French Marquise."

Having begun to accumulate French ill-wishers through his wizardry in romance and finance, Serge promptly began to add to their number a legion of Englishmen.

These new acquisitions included the management and the stockholders of Chosen Mining, Ltd., a London company that owned gold mines in Korea. It was a highly regarded concern in the City, England's financial center — a splendid investment for a young man who'd just made a million. But that's not what Serge planned to do with his bundle. Little Serge decided to rule giant Chosen by ruining it — an incredibly risky enterprise for any market mastermind except Serge.

He developed a method for eliminating risks that became known as "The Rubinstein Squeeze." That's how *Fortune*, the magazine of big business, described it in an obituary four months after his death. The article commemorated the unique position he had achieved in the big business community by managing simultaneously to deplore and eulogize his shady shrewdness. *Fortune's* readers learned the Rubinstein strategy for avoiding taking chances:

"I never speculated unless the elements of speculation were removed and I control or have the man who turns the wheels on my payroll."

Judging by his long and successful career, the strategy was foolproof. Viewing it in hindsight, from the way it ended, Serge had risked only one thing — his neck.

Of course, the tactics of controlling the wheels or the wheel-turners differed from operation to operation. In the case of Chosen Ltd., outsider Rubinstein found someone on the inside who sold him information on how Chosen's big wheels were turning off the straight and narrow. This valuable material he altruistically gave away free to the press. Bankers, brokers, and Chosen Corp. stockholders were appalled by the allegations of hanky-panky, which were denied by management, then confirmed by investigation. In the ensuing scandal, one board member went to jail for having had his hand in the company till. Others barely managed to stay out of prison.

Serge did not go unrewarded for exposing corruption. As Chosen's executives toppled, so did the stocks. When the latter were at their all-time low, Serge bought control of the immensely profitable company.

It is impossible to know just how many millions this maneuver made for Serge. Nor how many more people he had convinced the world would be a better place without him. If he had been killed then, in 1933, it would have made matters somewhat simpler for the police than they were in 1955. By then Serge had amassed an army of possible revengers, not only in the old world, but in the new.

The U.S.A. was not exactly a welcome wagon for a French reject. But it couldn't summarily shut out the affable, obviously affluent young newcomer who, despite all previous evidence of his Russian birth, suddenly turned out to have been born Portuguese. The passport he presented to the U.S. Immigration officers in 1938 was made out to and signed by the bearer, Serge Manuel Rubinstein de Ronello.

This bewildering transformation needed some fancy explanation, especially under oath. Serge-Manuel swore it wasn't a transformation. He'd always been Portuguese but he hadn't revealed it because he was guarding the family honor. Now he had no choice but to expose the skeleton in the Rubinstein-de Ronello closet. The awful truth was that his dear mother had sinned once, and...well...he was illegitimate...a love child...the product of a liaison between her and a Senhor de Ronello, a native Portuguese.

This soap opera stuff seems to have so fascinated the immigration fellows that they let Serge in. But the spell didn't last. In later episodes we find them trying to deport him. Serge fought them off for more than a decade with the best legal talent.money could buy, and a lot of surreptitious help from his friends.

It is possible that among the legion of Serge's intimates, some of them highly visible public figures, others who preferred anonymity, there were those who helped keep him in the country because they honestly felt he was a desirable alien. But from what we know of Serge, it is more likely favors were bought — with money or with information about where bodies were buried. In this kind of deal, what happens when the buyer feels he isn't getting his money's worth?

By January, 1955, time was running out in America for Serge. He was due to appear in court a month later for a deportation hearing. The word was out that nothing could help keep him here this time. He'd given proof of his undesirability with one conviction for draft-dodging and a narrow escape from a second for fraud. Moreover, Immigration had found proof that his Portuguese passport was a forgery. In all fairness, no amount of influence could help beat these raps.

Not notorious for his sense of fairness, Serge might well have put the squeeze on his friends. Always amply supplied with inside information, he might have threatened to put it to use. Would blackmail have been beyond Serge? Might it not have provoked the retaliatory, fatal squeeze on his neck? No concrete evidence. Merely a speculation which opens another can of possible suspects.

The animosities generated by Rubinstein's efforts to remain in the United States had

Rubinstein's body being carried from his mansion by the police.

other ramifications. Brother Andre, busy in the courts trying to nail his sibling as a crook, now sued for defamation of their mother's character. But Serge's preposterous claim to love-childhood seemed not to affect his tender relationship with his mother. She occupied the top floor bedroom of the quintuplex the night he was murdered. Another permanent member of the mansion was her sister.

Both elderly ladies did their best to assist the police investigation. Mrs. Rubinstein remembered hearing the sound of disputing voices from her son's quarters about 2 A.M. (The medical examiner established the time of death as between 2 and 5 A.M.) She had called down, but there was no answer.

Her eighty-two-year-old sister reported that she had awakened during the night and had seen "a mysterious woman" prowling through the hall. Investigation revealed that the mystery woman was really butler Worthy in a bathrobe, making his closing rounds. And the disputing voices Mrs. Rubinstein heard only confirmed that it was not unusual for Serge to have secret meetings in the wee hours with anonymous visitors of both sexes.

Early on, Homicide concluded that the butler didn't do it, nor the members of the household staff, nor his ex-wife, living in California. They also eliminated robbery as a motive. Valuables were not taken, nor was there any sign of a forcible entry. Having eliminated these possibilities, the logical conclusion was that the killer was someone on close enough terms with Serge to gain admission to the mansion.

But who? Unearthing Serge's personal and private list of names and addresses should have helped the detectives. Ordinarily a victim's little black book gives investigators a lead to his intimate private life — to possible suspects. The trouble with Serge's list was that it was contained not in one pocket-sized book but in three enormous looseleaf ledgers, inscribed with hundreds of names. The police never made the contents of these volumes public. It's doubtful whether doing so would have helped them in any way, and it was certain that it would have embarrassed a lot of people who had a lot of clout.

None of the prominent personages with whom Serge had mingled rushed forward to help the authorities revenge their "friend." He was gone and forgotten. Among those absent at his funeral were the guests who glittered at his lavish wedding reception in Washington. Among those present, the gossip columnists reported, were nine Ambassadors, dozens of Senators and Representatives, scores of lobbyists, political bosses, scads of screen and stage stars, scions of society, high and cafe, and Wall Street luminaries too numerous to count.

As for the shadowy types he had on his secret payroll, you couldn't realistically expect them to mourn his passing in public. The police would have welcomed an opportunity to chat with any of his stable of inside informers.

For instance, the guy who had tipped him off that New York City was going to take over the BMT subway. Or the one who'd slipped him the advance dope about the merger between Western Union and Postal Telegraph. Serge had bragged about the killings he had made on these deals. But he never revealed his sources.

Had they been located they would have soared to the top of the suspect list. In the annals of bribery it is not unprecedented for the bribed to demand a larger cut of the swag, be refused, and get violent. Could be that on the agenda of Serge's last meeting was a motion to divide the profits more equally on some deal and Serge had voted it down.

Despite arduous police efforts, this rich field for investigation did not live up to its potential. The detectives cannot be criticized for not striking pay dirt. *Fortune* magazine's expert researchers, who dug for the facts about Rubinstein's deals, could come up with only what he had put on record. And they disclaimed any responsibility for the accuracy of his statements.

When a victim is an ex-convict, an obvious place to look for clues is among jailbirds. The reasoning is simple. A man with a criminal past is likely to have a criminal present. It is reasonable to assume that among the underworld characters with whom Serge exercised in the prison yard, were some capable of murder.

This may have been why the only business associate of Rubinstein to speak to the press, stockbroker Stanley K. Stanley, told reporters: "I believe it was a mob job." But Mr. Stanley also reaffirmed that to his knowledge Serge had many business enemies.

There were suspects of both kinds connected with Serge's imprisonment in Lewisburg Penitentiary in 1947. Serge was convicted for a new dodge, avoiding the World War II draft. There were plenty of other draft dodgers, but none of them in his evasive class.

Before the jury found him guilty he had managed to have his 1A classification — immediately available for service — changed fifteen times. While one set of wires were being pulled to keep him in the country, another set was tugging him out of the Army.

According to Mr. Stanley, Rubinstein's reluctance to serve was because "he was a neutral." But he couldn't have been all that neutral. One of his claims to deferment was that he was indispensable to the American war effort on the home production front, as the owner of the Taylorcraft Corporation, which made airplanes.

The court, however, judged his purchase of Taylorcraft a phony scheme to stay out of uniform. Not only was Serge convicted, but the president of Taylorcraft, whom he involved, was found guilty of complicity in the fraud and also went to jail. Though he was probably a willing conspirator he could certainly not have had much affection for Serge.

In the last year of his life Serge was involved in several newsworthy happenings which he wouldn't talk about. He was beaten up by two men whom he could not or would not identify. And unidentified sources told reporters that they saw Serge chase a man into a telephone booth and throw thousand dollar bills at him.

The police had less trouble authenticating the gossip item that Rubinstein had escorted seven beautiful women to the New Year's Eve White Russian Ball, just weeks before he was murdered.

This last event, a flamboyant example of Serge's prowess as a Casanova, put the murder in the sensational category of a crime of passion. None of the other facts of his life which were laid bare were as absorbing to the public.

It should be mentioned that for his last eight years he was a bachelor, his wife having divorced him in 1947 for punching her around.

Since the police were only human, they gave this aspect of his career particular attention. They discovered that Serge rarely confined his attentions to fewer than a half-dozen women at one time. He had a habit of

Serge Rubinstein's mansion on Fifth Avenue, where he was found dead.

providing his favorites with keys to his front door, and when he changed them for a new batch, he changed the lock.

The discards were of obvious interest because everybody hates being rejected. But of more immediate interest was the then current crop of key holders. They could let themselves in. Likewise, anyone who could borrow, coerce, or steal one of these keys, could get into the house.

In this love interest or key phase of the investigation, the police established that the last person to be seen with the victim was model Estelle Gardner. She had supped and danced with Serge at a very exclusive and exceptionally expensive night spot, Nino's La Rue. A cab driver who had picked them up there remembered the time, 12:30 A.M., and he had no trouble remembering his fares because Serge had borrowed a quarter from him to tip Nino's doorman. He said he'd driven his fares to 814 Fifth, and saw them enter the house.

Miss Gardner took the story up from there. Yes, she'd been with Serge until 1:30 A.M. for a nightcap, and then had gone home. And she proved it. The police questioned Pat Wray, another of Serge's companions, and heard from her that at 2:30 A.M. Serge had phoned and invited her to drop over. She had respectfully declined the invitation. And that was the last time anyone heard from him. Sometime during the next two to three hours he was killed.

The fifty detectives assigned to the case had the pleasure of meeting some five hundred beautiful women before they finished checking out the harem listings in Serge's address books. But that's all they got from the discarded woman-jealous boyfriend theory.

Then came an anonymous tip that set Homicide off on the trail of crime-for-profit suspects. BREAKTHROUGH IN RUBE STRANGLING, the tabloids screamed. POLICE HOLD EX CON. ADMITS SERGE SNATCH SCHEME.

It looked bad for felon Herman Scholz. Though his was the only suspect name not included in Serge's address book, he became Rubinstein enemy Number 1 in the press and in the District Attorney's office. The fifty-year-old, jockey-sized, part-time hire-a-car chauffeur had a big small-time criminal record. When the police broke into his home they discovered an arsenal — sub-machine guns, pistols, revolvers, blackjacks, and switchblades.

Scholz told a pretty unlikely story. He professed to have collected the lethal gadgets because he was planning to rob a bank: The skeptical cops couldn't connect the shooting irons to the Rubinstein killing, but they had another link, at once less lethal and more sinister.

Stashed away in Scholz's room, along with the armament, was a bundle of clippings reporting in detail the mystery of the murder in the mansion. Of course, there's no law that says a person can't cut up a newspaper. But the police hammered away at this pastime of Scholz's.

Scholz finally confessed that another of his ambitions was to kidnap Serge and hold him for ransom. Moreover, he admitted that he had taken steps to put the plan into practice. For three months he had been watching the Rubinstein mansion.

Scholz was held as a material witness on $25,000 bail. A spokesman for the District Attorney's office proclaimed: "Scholz conveyed his kidnapping plan to persons, members of the underworld, who in our very definite opinion committed the murder."

Scholz did not deny he had conveyed his plan to colleagues, but he swore they had rejected him and his dream of the big time. He was only saving the clippings to show the scoffers what a golden opportunity they had missed. They'd been beaten to the punch by the murder. The authorities thought that the accused hadn't told all. Judge Jonah J. Goldstein peered down from his bench at the diminutive dreamer and said:

"You're too small to have tried kidnapping by yourself."

(Previous to this legal opinion there had been no height requirement for kidnapping.)

As time passed, Assistant D.A. Alexander Herman began to hedge the prosecutor's first firm conviction.

"As to what we have now, it looks like an

underworld job, a snatch which went wrong."

And that's where the matter rested in 1955, and where it still rests. The snatch theory got no further than the passion theory.

Murder mystery fans generally enjoy an after-the-fact advantage over real or fictional detectives. They can usually prove they're smarter than the professionals by picking out the flaws in police procedures which prevented the solution of the crime.

In the Rubinstein case the amateur detective is as stumped as the one who gets paid. The New York police asked the right questions, beginning with: "Who had a motive for killing Serge? Did he have any enemies?" And that's about as far as they or anyone else could get.

To achieve his pre-eminent position as a candidate for murder, Serge had campaigned all his life. There were just too many people whom he had given persuasive reasons to vote for his death. There were just too many suspects.

The Rubinstein murderer remained free, not because he'd carefully covered up his crime, but because he had an accomplice — the victim. By a lifetime of accumulating potential murderers, Serge made it impossible to solve his murder. If justice was never done, well, there's a kind of justice in that.

THE TEN HOT OLD MASTERS

Almost every occupation, vocation, and pro-
fession has its time-tested how-to-succeed
rules. And there are all kinds of schools and
colleges where ambitious young people can
learn the prescribed way to shinny up the
ropes to the top. Relatively new among such
institutions of learning are the academies in
which career-minded policemen study how to
circumvent robbers.

So far as can be ascertained, there are no
accredited institutions of learning for robbers, unless you include prisons where the
course of study is less than formal. But even
without textbooks, would-be masters of the
criminal arts learn to practice the basic rules
of how-not-to-be-caught by the police.

Although police and criminals have opposing goals, the activities of both sides are guided by identical rules — like any contest. Police game plans are based on the regulation do's and don't's of their opponents, and vice versa.

Among the fundamentals learned by both teams is that the safest way to succeed at stealing is — steal money, provided it's not in large denominations. All cash is green, not identifiable; possession and/or use of dollars, unlike, say, marijuana, is not a crime.

All other loot is less cool. Hot stuff requires the services of a middleman, a fence who discounts the value of the goods, whether they're precious gems or bonds or TV sets. He in turn seeks a customer for whom the price has to be right. This class of consumer is bound to be more picky about a purchase than even Ralph Nader. During such transactions, no matter how gingerly the merchandise is handled, all concerned can get burned.

Nevertheless there are some criminals who violate accepted rules with impunity. Mostly they don't get caught, though they specialize in acquiring the hottest, most easily identifiable, least salable loot there is — rare, one-of-a-kind, works of art.

On the plus side of stealing paintings, there's something to be said. Once out of the frame they're easily transported. Canvas doesn't weigh much, can be rolled, folded, tucked out of sight under almost any clothing other than a bikini. It's true that a masterpiece in square inches is generally worth less than the work of the same artist done in feet, but it's worth stealing.

For example, the largest of the ten paintings stolen from the Brooklyn Museum in 1933 was 24" by 18". But one of them, *The Ascension of Christ* by Peter Paul Rubens, might bring some three million dollars on the open market — if it were available.

The Brooklyn Museum robbery is a kind of classic example of evil doing in the art world. One sign is how simple it was. Another is the extent to which the police were baffled. They weren't even able to find someone they could suspect unjustly. Still another is that after they had succeeded at first, the crooks for some reason tried again, and again — twice more, fruitlessly. Of course, it might not have been the same mob. The police were never sure. There was some reason to think yes, and some to think no.

The first clue that there was something amiss at the Brooklyn Museum was a rope dangling from a fourth story window to the ground. Precisely how long it had been there, in view of the headlights of cars rolling along Washington Avenue, nobody knows. Perhaps if some passerby or motorist had seen it, he would have thought it had something to do with the work construction men were engaged in.

Noticed it was, finally, at 3 A.M. Sunday, April 30, 1933, by alert night watchman Frank

The Ascension of Christ by Peter Paul Rubens.

Walsh, one of the eight after-hours guardians of the Museum's treasures. Mr. Walsh discovered that the rope was anchored to a newel post on the fourth floor landing. With his colleagues he searched the fourth floor gallery. Nothing was missing. In strict observance of the institution's regulations, he reported the happening in writing.

The Walsh report was put where it belonged, on the desk of his boss, Museum executive Joseph Seabeck. Mr. Seabeck had Sunday off, and thus didn't get to read it until some time on Monday. His superior, Director William Fox, was at his post when the Museum opened at 2:00 P.M. Sunday, but nobody thought to tell him about the mysterious rope.

It wasn't until 3:00 P.M. on Sunday, that fifth floor gallery attendant Charles Hansen noticed that ten of the frames hanging on the walls of his turf were empty. What took so long is hard to explain. In justice to him, it should be pointed out that his job was to look out for people inclined to steal paintings, not to look at paintings.

At any rate, before Fox learned of the theft, and somebody remembered the rope, and a connection was made, much time had passed. Too much time, in the angry opinion of Deputy Chief Inspector Vincent J. Sweeney. He complained that the police department wasn't informed until the next day. The press reported:

DELAY OVER ROPE CLUE
CHECKS ART RECOVERY

In the Chief's own words, "The trail is cold."

Of course the trail was more chilly than it would have been with instant notification. But there is reason to suspect that Sweeney might have been copping a premature plea. He laid heavy stress upon the difficulties his men faced:

"There has been only a meager description of the suspects."

In fact there was less than a meager description. There was none at all. Nobody had seen or heard anything suspicious. There were fingerprints on the vacated frames, but they were so jumbled as to be useless.

This did not prevent the police from coming up with some highly theoretical suspects, good for a headline:

INTERNATIONAL CROOKS
GET MUSEUM TREASURE

Any particular crooks? The police couldn't be more specific than:

"A band of art thieves in touch with markets (unspecified) and collectors (unnamed) all over the world."

They had reason to believe — they didn't give it — it was the same gang that had stolen five rare miniatures from New York's Metropolitan Museum of Art in 1927. In that case, the modus operandi had been different. The crooks had also walked off with the frames. That was only because the Met's frames were studded with real diamonds, the police noted, to explain the discrepancy.

Sweeney also credited this company of super-thieves with having scored against galleries, museums, and private collections in European capitals. But despite all the hypothetical accomplishments of this hypothetical gang, the police were far from helpless, Sweeney assured the press:

"The department is equipped to carry on the hunt for the treasures through the education of Detective Lieutenant Thomas Dugan who has been studying to become an art connoisseur since the theft of the Metropolitan paintings."

Without withdrawing his endorsement of Lt. Dugan, whom he had borrowed from a Manhattan precinct, Sweeney cautioned against optimism:

"Art thefts generally take many years for solution. Art thieves are the cleverest in the world."

There is much in what the chief said. The folks who specialize in art thievery have achieved a distinction matched by no other evil-doers. They have their own magazine — a publication exclusively devoted to stolen works of art.

It is the brainchild of an enterprising French businessman who seized the opportunity presented by the regularity with which art treasures keep disappearing. Called *The Official International of Stolen Paintings and Objects of Art*, it is to art fanciers what *Sports*

Illustrated is to sports fans. Museums, galleries, private collectors all over the world subscribe — fifty dollars annually — for its descriptions and photographs of stolen art treasures.

Police were nagged by reporters to explain inexplicable circumstances, and they properly passed the buck to the Museum officials. A curator, cornered by the press with: "Why did it take the fifth floor guard so long to discover the paintings were missing?", answered with a condensed course in art history:

"Pictures have often been hung upside down in galleries and neither the public nor attendants have noticed." This doesn't seem to say much for pictures, the public, the attendants, or for that matter the curators who hang exhibits.

Though the police theories of who did the deed were vague, they were on much firmer ground with the hypothesis of how it was done.

Deduction: The thieves had entered the premises along with less acquisitive art lovers on Saturday and had stayed over after closing in any number of possible hiding places.

Deduction: There were at least three malefactors in the Museum. Evidence? The sixty-foot rope was found to be made up of three twenty-foot segments. It followed that each crook had entered the building with his segment wound around under his clothing.

Mystery: Why did they take these particular pictures? Conjecture: They had an order from a particular buyer. Or they could be such consummate connoisseurs that they selected works they knew were in demand by many no-questions-asked buyers.

It was Sweeney's opinion that since the works were foreign made, patriotic foreign dealers might be eager to buy them on the grounds that they were being returned to where they came from.

National pride has been an established motive for art theft since the heisting of the *Mona Lisa* from the Louvre in 1911. The Louvre is of course French. But the smiling lady of the portrait is Italian. And the fifteenth-century master, Leonardo Da Vinci, who painted the most famous grimace of all time on her face, was Italian. The unregenerate thief was Italian too. When caught, he proudly proclaimed:

"I would be unworthy of Italy if I did not try to return to her this masterpiece. I did it to revenge Napoleon's depredations on Italian art."

The New York police may have had patriotic reasons for assigning the blame to foreigners. When a bunch of paintings was taken from Buckingham Palace in 1930, the English press charged it was the work of American crooks conspiring with conscienceless American art dealers.

The Brooklyn Museum haul came at an

inauspicious time for the police. It was the climax of a series of raids on New York's high-toned art alley — the East 57th Street galleries. None of the treasures had been recovered. There were no arrests. The gallery owners were furious.

Another giant-sized headache for the art-theft fellows was their inability to explain the mystery around the invaluable original manuscript of Sir Walter Scott's *Lady of the Lake*. They were stumped when it was lifted from the Morgan Library. But it was even more stupefying when the precious document suddenly reappeared in the library after a six-month absence.

So the police tried very hard. Interrogating all 125 employees of the Museum got them nowhere. Descriptions of the missing ten were cabled to European authorities. Ports of exit were watched. Intense attention was paid to the only evidence — beside the empty frames — that crime had been committed, the egress rope.

Who'd be most likely to employ this hazardous method of escape? Logically, persons with a special kind of athletic ability and training. This suggested acrobats or aerialists. Where are they most likely to be found? Under the big top. These propositions were supported by the discovery that the rope was the kind used in circuses. Find the circus to which it belonged and you're on the way to a solution of the burglary.

Unfortunately, the rope lead didn't prove out. As Captain James Pritchard, Sweeney's second in command, explained:

"It is also the sort of rope used in shifting stage scenery, in dumbwaiters, in dry cleaning establishments, and in flag halyards, though such halyards are not usually that thick."

Ringling Bros. & Barnum & Bailey went uninvestigated while thirty detectives probed antique stores, obscure galleries, and junk shops. Ten more, under the supervision of Lt. Dugan, enlisted the services of the U.S. Secret Service and U.S. Customs inspectors to scrutinize vessels departing from New York harbor.

Two weeks after the theft, Director Fox advertised a reward of two thousand dollars for the arrest and conviction of the crooks. Recovery of the plunder was not included. There was no response to the offer.

Meanwhile, the Museum took steps to make sure it couldn't happen again. All employees were ordered to shape up. With all possible security precautions taken, the Museum was to be invulnerable — well, almost invulnerable, as time would prove.

Three months after the first robbery, a second attempt was made. The fourth floor gallery watchman spotted a shadowy intruder, sounded the alarm and gave chase. The would-be robber beat him down the stairs and escaped out of an open window. All that the police could learn from the winded watchman was that the suspect was about twenty-five years old, and toted a pistol.

Obviously the police had reason to wonder if there was a connection between incursions one and two. Was the second intruder a member of the same band? Or was he an amateur inspired by the success of the professionals? Whatever the answers were, it was embarrassing.

Just forty-eight hours later, the underworld was again guilty of contempt for the police. Once again, in the dead of night, there was somebody in the fourth floor gallery for no good reason. His stealthy footsteps were overheard by an alert guard who tiptoed to a telephone to call the police. In answer, a hundred on- and off-duty police surrounded the building. But the quarry was as vigilant as the hunters. He got away without being seen. Once again out of an open window. Once again down a dangling rope — the same length and make of rope the thieves slid down in caper number one.

What could the men in blue do but suffer in silence and worry about the possibility of number four? And there was indeed going to be another robbery at the Museum, but it wouldn't happen till long after Sweeney, Dugan, et al, had retired — not until 1974.

While the police were still puzzling over the triple mystery, public interest lapsed. The curious crowds who came to visit the scene of

ART THIEVES RAID BROOKLYN MUSEUM

Ten Old Masters, Eight From Friedsam Collection, Taken During Week-End.

WORLD ALARM IS SENT OUT

Dangling Rope Is Left by the Invaders—Fingerprints of Two Found on Window.

A daring week-end theft of paintings from the Brooklyn Museum was revealed yesterday by Dr. William H. Fox, director of that institution, who asked the police to broadcast an international alarm for the thieves and their loot.

Ten paintings, eight of them from the valuable collection of the late Colonel Michael Friedsam, were taken from the fifth floor galleries. They were valued at about $35,000 and were not insured.

A sixty-foot length of rope, knotted fast to a newel post on the fourth floor of the building at the Washington Avenue end and extending to the ground, gave a hint of the manner in which the thieves escaped. Fingerprints on the window sill indicated that two men committed the crime, the most sensational of its kind in years.

The stolen pictures included examples of the work of such noted early French painters as François Clouet, who is said to have modeled the death masks of Francis I and Henry II, and of Jean Fouquet, who is considered by connoisseurs the most representative of the fifteenth century painters.

Story on the front page of *The New York Times,* May 2, 1933, reporting the theft.

the crime stopped coming. The empty frames were taken down, and the spaces filled with ten other paintings of similar sizes from the Museum's collection. Then, two years after the original theft, the story broke into the press again. In the interim, Director Fox had been succeeded by his assistant, Philip N. Youtz.

The new director let it be known that there was no need to look any further than the Museum storerooms for four of the pictures. He confessed that the quartet had been secretly hidden there shortly after they were reported stolen.

Yes, he admitted to newsman, the Museum had been deceiving the public, but it was a necessary deception, and the police were in on it. And so were the thieves.

The conspiracy of silence had been maintained for two years because each of the participants had his own special self-interest in keeping mum. The Museum wanted the paintings back. The police wanted the robbers. The robbers didn't want the police, but they seemed eager to restore the paintings to their rightful owner. Had they repented? Gone straight? Why else had they returned forty percent of their ill-gotten gains?

Well, with all the crazy rule-breaking, there had been a method to their madness. They'd never intended to exert themselves unloading the loot. They had a ready-made buyer in mind all the time — the Brooklyn Museum.

Once Director Youtz made clear the robbery had been a kidnapping (such ventures came to be known as "artnappings"), the reappearance of the four fell into line. They'd been returned as proof that the ransom seekers held the other, far more valuable, six.

The gang was so hip about art that they knew three of the pictures were only "attributed to" old masters. That is, art experts weren't certain whether the artists to whom they were credited had painted them. And the fourth, though not an "attributed to" work, was that of a lesser painter. These four, which were not in the same high-priced league as the others, were those the Museum had secreted.

Youtz revealed that the first ransom note offered to restore the four for free. And it set a low, quick turnover sale price for the remaining six — $38,000. Like people-kidnappers, they ordered the Museum not to tell the police.

Naturally, the Museum told the police, who instructed them to seem to follow the gang's instructions. Accordingly, a personal ad in the press informed the crooks that they had a deal.

The gang's second note outlined the next steps. Enclosed was a key to a locker in Pennsylvania Station. Enclosed in the locker would be four paintings. If satisfied with paintings, leave package of $38,000 over specified newsstand in 42nd Street station of IRT subway.

Key in hand, Youtz, shadowed unobtrusively by plainclothesmen, went to Pennsylvania Station. Pulses pounding, he opened the locker, and extracted the canvases. There were the four as promised. Indubitably they were the real articles. He could not help looking around for someone acting suspiciously. But in the crowd of commuters he saw no such person. Nor did the police.

So far, so good. All that remained, to recover the rest of the plunder, was to follow the rest of the instructions.

Youtz did. Except for two details. The bundle he put on the newsstand was a dummy. And it had been wired. The moment a finger was laid on it, lights would flash where the police had been staked out.

It was a very ingenious trap. The lawmen had the newsstand surrounded. The robbers couldn't possibly know the package was a phony, or wired, until they touched it. And then it would be too late.

The only trouble was that nobody ever fingered the bundle, or came anywhere near it.

The most reasonably obvious explanation for the no-show is that the gang had somehow gotten wise. But there is much in the annals of art theft that isn't reasonable or obvious. A thief has been known to take a masterpiece for profit, and then became so enamored of it that he wouldn't part with it for any sum of money. This sort of eccentricity may not make much sense to anyone but a true art appreciator. For that matter, only real connoiseurs of art have any business in the stealing end of it.

When you come right down to it the activities of the legitimate inhabitants of the art world are hardly less idiosyncratic than those of the illegitimate. It's hard for laymen to understand the unconventional behavior of so many great painters. What makes one oil-covered canvas priceless, and another not worth the canvas it's painted on? If it's the judgment of the critics that makes a masterpiece, then how come so many authenticated masterpieces turn out to be forgeries? If the acknowledged experts are so expert, why is it that so many have so often been wrong in evaluating the work of new artists? What kind of know-how is it that makes it impossible for a work to be given away — a painting that later costs more than most millionaires can afford?

The fact is that art, like beauty of all kinds, is in the eye of the beholder. And unless you're in the art trade as a dealer or collector, curator or crook, you don't have to know anything about art to know what you like to look at.

The reason it took Director Youtz two years to come clean with press and public, was that he had been trying desperately to resume negotiations with the gang. There were ads pleading for forgiveness, pledging to deal this time in good faith. But there'd been no peep out of the kidnappers. His confession was an admission that he'd given up hope. Thus, the curtain came down on an unhappy ending to the 1933 occurrences at the Brooklyn Museum.

It took a long time before the police came to the Museum again. To be precise, forty-one years and seven months from the time a rope was dangled out of a window.

Art-crook history repeated itself on December 31, 1974. Michael Botwinick, now the director in Brooklyn, informed the police that somebody had somehow walked off with master painter Auguste Renoir's *Still Life With Blue Cup*: a small, easily transportable, one-of-a-kind work of French impressionism, valued at $50,000.

Back in '33, the Director Fox, harassed by misfortune, plagued by reporters about his less-than-tight security, defended himself with:

"Anything out of the ordinary is not agreeable. But no institution run by human beings is infallible."

Botwinick would have had to agree. With modern burglar-proof alarm systems, and with all the most up-to-date security measures, the Brooklyn Museum was yet human. So humanly fallible that Botwinick had never even heard of the first robbery. Apparently, as successive generations of directors handed over the reins, the word of the missing masterpieces was not passed along.

Of course, in 1974 things were different. There was a new generation of policemen, and one must assume a new generation of robbers. There was no rope clue, no open window. And if there has been a ransom note, it has been kept secret.

But the more some things change, the more they remain the same. Like the first time, there were no prints, no suspects. Current art-theft expert Detective Robert Volpe alerted the U.S. Customs Service as had his predecessor, and added Interpol and the FBI. Photographs of the missing Renoir have been sent to authorities abroad and at home. What luck Volpe will have remains to be seen.

But in some high art circles there is considerable optimism, judging by an announcement in the *New York Times*:

"To fill the Brooklyn's temporary gap, the Metropolitan Museum of Art has lent it the artist's *The Bay of Naples* until the stolen work is recovered."

One can only hope that the Renoir gap will be less temporary than the six spaces left on Brooklyn's walls two score and one year ago.

THE MAN WITH
THE MONKEY NOSE

When the burglar alarm clanged in Holmes
Van Brunt's Long Island mansion, he woke
with a start, swore at the prospect of going out
into the pre-dawn storm, and sleepily groped
for his pants. He hadn't the remotest idea that
he was about to bring to an end the search for
the criminals believed to be responsible for
the first kidnapping in America.

All that he knew was that something, wind
or rain, or someone, had tripped the warning
system in his brother's shuttered summer
home, and he'd better take a look-see. He
roused his son, his gardener, and his hired
man, and though he was almost certain a short
circuit had set off the bells, he took precautions. Armed with shotguns and pistols, the
four men went reluctantly out into the freez-

ing blackness of the December downpour to investigate.

As they slogged toward the adjacent house, they saw the faint beams of two lanterns moving through the empty rooms. They cocked their weapons and prepared to ambush the robbers when they emerged with their loot. But the housebreakers were doing a thorough, leisurely job. Time passed and the watchers got wetter and colder, and so impatient that they decided to enter the house. They were heard. The lanterns went out. The intruders ran.

They were met by a fusillade of gunfire. The shooting stopped when both of the robbers were down. One was dead. The other, a younger man, was bleeding from many wounds. Told by Van Brunt that he was dying, he gasped that he was Joe Douglas, his dead companion was Bill Mosher, and that together they had kidnapped little Charley Brewster Ross. Before he could say any more, he was dead.

Headlines shouted that the kidnapping of July 1, 1874, had finally been solved. Though everyone was certain these were the wanted men, witnesses were brought to the morgue to view the corpses. The only eyewitness to the actual crime was a six-year-old boy, Charley's brother, Walter. Never having looked at death, Walter was terrified. But he manfully identified Mosher, the man he had described as "monkey nose," and Douglas as the two who took him and his little brother for a ride to buy firecrackers.

It is at least questionable whether a judge and jury would have found Mosher and Douglas guilty since the case against them rested so heavily on the testimony of a child. But even if they were the kidnappers, the mystery was not solved by their death, for Charley Ross was never found.

The case of Charley Ross was a tragedy of errors from the very beginning. Mistakes made by the good people from the best of motives; mistakes made by the bad people from the worst of motives. The trouble was that neither the law nor the lawbreakers had had any experience with this sort of crime. Nobody had ever held a child for ransom in America before.

Those were innocent years, the 1880's. Of course there were crimes of passion and for profit. And there were instances of Fagins who spirited children away and taught them the thief trade. There were tales without proof of wandering gypsy tribes who stole children. Boys and girls did disappear, but these were slum children. Not much fuss was ever made about their disappearance.

Charley Ross, however, was an upper-middle class boy. He was taken from an elite section of Philadelphia. His father, Christian K. Ross, was a very substantial citizen, a prominent merchant, one of Philadelphia's first families. The Ross economic and social posi-

62

The little kidnapped boy Charley Ross.

tion was the key to the case — for their peers reasoned that if it could happen to the Rosses it could happen to them. That must be prevented at all costs.

Kidnapping was so inconceivable to Ross and the rest of his class that until the ransom note was received, three days after the boy disappeared, they believed he had just strayed away. A reward was offered for "a lost small boy with long curly flaxen hair, hazel eyes, round face, dressed in a brown linen suit with short skirt, broad brimmed hat and laced shoes."

The police assumption that Charley was lost seems naive for even those unsophisticated days. They knew from Walter that two nice men in a horse and buggy had taken him and Charley for a ride, and dropped him off with a quarter in his hand to buy fireworks in a cigar store while they waited for him. Walter said when he came out with his purchase, the two nice men and his brother were gone. He looked all over for the buggy, couldn't find it anywhere, and started to cry. The story was continued by a passerby who saw the weeping child and returned him to his home, where Ross was scouring the neighborhood in search of his missing sons.

In the opinion of the police, the two men had taken the boys for a jaunt in an excess of pre-Fourth of July, high alcoholic spirits. They calmed the distracted Ross by assuring him that as soon as the merrymakers sobered up they would return Charley with shamefaced apologies. By the second day the drunken lark theory was supplemented by a hypothesis that the men had been ashamed to return Charley, had let him off somewhere, and he was being kept by some citizen who would want recompense for returning him. The police urged Ross to relax. The reward offer would bring Charley home.

While Ross was trying to be patient, Dr. Walker, a Germantown physician, confirmed Walter's description of the two men. He reported that on his rounds he had seen two men parked in a buggy near the Ross house. He hadn't paid too much attention, but he had noticed that the older man had a somewhat deformed nose. Till then the police had not paid much attention to Walter's "man with a monkey nose."

Walker's information that the men had been casing the premises made the police junk their previous theories. Yet, they could think of no reason for the men to have taken the boy, except perhaps that Ross had some enemy who wanted to make trouble for him. But try as hard as he could, Ross could think of no one whom he could have given any reason to take his son.

Then on July 4th the first ransom note came. It was the beginning of a correspondence that marked a new era in crime. Ross and the police read it unbelievingly. No one had ever received or for that matter written such a letter before. It said:

"July 3. Mr. Ros be not uneasy you son charly bruster be al writ we is got him and no power on earth can deliver out of our hand — You will hav two pay us befor you git him from us an pay us a big cent to — if you put the cops hunting for him you is only defeeting yu own end we is got him fix so no living power can gits him from us alive if any aproch is maid to his hidin place that is the signil for his instant anihilation — if yu regard his lif puts no one to search for him you money can fech him out alive an no other existin powers don't deceve yuself and think the detectives can hit him from us for that is one imposebel you here from us in a few day"

There it was in black and white. Inconceivable, unprecedented, monstrous. The illiterate scrawl announced a new era in crime. Christian Ross reacted as any father would. He read the letter in fear for his son's life. He wanted him back no matter what. The police responded differently. The ransom demand read to them as a threat, not only against little Charley but as a threat against all children of moneyed parents. If it were paid, no child would be safe. Paramount in their minds was catching and punishing the criminals. Of course, it was implicit that when they found the criminals they would also find Charley.

As a good citizen, Christian Ross had to go along. He had already, though innocently, ignored the notes warning against involving the police. Though he took the threat of Charley's "instant anihilation" to heart, he was a pillar of Philadelphia society, and he saw justice in

July 3

Mr. Ros— be not uneasy you son charly bruster be al writ we is got him and no powers on earth can deliver out of our hand— you wil hav two pay us befor you git him from us— an pay us a big cent to— if you put the cops hunting for him you is only defeeting you own end—

A facsimile of one of the letters to Mr. Ross from the kidnappers.

the police approach. He could not let his individual self-interest take precedence over the general interest of his peers.

Besides, the police were certain to find his boy. They had ordered the most intensive search of the city ever conducted. Ferries, depots, barns, stables; any remotely suspicious person, place, vehicle would be investigated. In the light of this dragnet, it seemed that the kidnappers' boast, "no powers can deliver [Charley] out of our hand," was ridiculous. The odds against the malefactors were tremendous. Hundreds of policemen in uniform, detectives in civilian dress, aroused citizens of Philadelphia were hunting for them. At the very least they would be forced to release the child.

But the strenuous day and night effort of the police and their allies got nowhere. Some people were beginning to believe the kidnappers would never be heard from again when, on July 8, the second note was delivered to Ross' store downtown. The price for the return of Charley was "20000 not one doler lest...."

Although the criminals had taken the child of a prominent, presumably affluent merchant, Ross did not have $20,000 nor anything like that. The depression of 1873 had struck him severely. He was in debt, close to bankruptcy, and his elaborate home was an attempt to keep up appearances. It is entirely possible that if Ross had had the money, he would have paid the ransom despite the police.

The police reasoned that if the kidnappers understood there would be no money given them, they would let the boy go. The flaw in this reasoning for Ross was the letter's "if yu love money more than child yu be its murderer not us for the money we will heve if we don't get from yu we be sure to get it from someone els for we wil make example of yure child that others may be wiser."

The threat to make an example of Charley, so that other parents would pay future demands, only strengthened the authorities' conviction that the ransom should not be paid. They were still confident that they would apprehend the criminals and rescue the child. Though Ross was much less confident, he went along.

In accord with the strategy worked out with the police and a committee of city leaders, Ross followed the second letter's instructions. He inserted an ad in the *Philadelphia Ledger* which appeared the following morning:

"Ros we be ready to negotiate."

Of course the strategists had no intention of negotiating. They were playing for time. While they were waiting to hear from the kidnappers, they intensified their efforts to find them. So sure were the law enforcers that they'd lay hands on the criminals that they made no attempt to conceal their duplicity. Though the wanted men read the dragnet stories in the press, and saw the posters which were prominently displayed not only in Philadelphia but in New York, they held still for it.

In note #3 they wrote Ross:

"use the detectives as yu pleas but dont let them mislede yu to the sacrifice of Charley."

The committee read this as backwatering, as a sign that the kidnappers' original threats against the boy's life were not to be taken seriously. But try as he could to be reasonable, Christian Ross was increasingly frightened. His efforts to reassure his wife, Sarah, that everything would be all right, failed because he himself didn't believe it. And so for the first time in his life he rebelled against the establishment he had unfailingly supported.

The object of the next meeting between Ross and the committee was to decide how to deal with the third note's demand that an ad be placed in which Ross would say:

"Ros wil come to terms" or "Ros wil not come to terms."

Ross told the committee that he had decided to come to terms; that he was going to borrow the $20,000 ransom, and get his son back. But now he ran into the committee's stern warning that if he did he would be compounding a felony. That was the law. For a man like Ross, to whom respect for law and order was as natural as breathing, this information was shattering. He could defy the counsel of his peers and the police, but not the immutable law.

With a heavy heart he surrendered to the dictates of the meeting. The personal he ran in the press in answer to note #3 hedged:

"Ros will come to terms to the extent of his ability."

The kidnapping was a sensational, front-page, continued story in the newspapers. The missing child's parents were hounded by reporters who ferreted out Ross' abortive rebellion against the authorities. Editorials in New York and Philadelphia took an outraged, vehement stand on the side of law and order. The ransom must not be paid. The criminals would not dare to harm Charley. Ross must put himself entirely in the hands of the police who would certainly catch the criminals.

Though he was increasingly isolated from public opinion, and dutifully followed the directives of the authorities, Ross also continued to make secret efforts to borrow the $20,000 among his friends.

The police followed up clues that poured in from well-meaning citizens. Gypsies, tramps, suspicious-looking members of the so-called criminal classes were arrested, interrogated, then released.

The procedures the police were following were standard, tested, proved by their experience in dealing with crime. But this was the first case of its kind, and their years of accumulated know-how did not work. In regard to kidnapping, they were amateurs. But for that matter this was a first for the criminals, too. They were also amateurs. This is reflected by the fact that they continued to negotiate, thus allowing the delay to continue, and making their capture more likely.

That the kidnappers were aware of their danger is made clear in their fourth letter: "is it necessary to repeat the fatle consequences of delaying to give time to detectives to find his hidin place." But they set no time limit. Instead, they put it up to Ross. They asked, "how much time yu want to obtain this money." And, extraordinarily, they spoke as reasonable businessmen to a fellow businessman, making a deal. "Ros this undertaken cost us $1000 to prepare the machinery to perform the work." This has the sound of a salesman explaining why the price for his goods is not unreasonable.

On the ninth day of Charley's disappearance, Ross, in ever deepening despair, qualified the reply to letter #4. He had been told to advertise: "Ros i is got it and be wilin to pay it." Though he took literally the blunt "we want no other anser and on the fath of yu word his lif hang," he consented to the police decision to respond: "Ros is wiling; have not got it; am doing my best to raise it."

Until this fourth interchange of correspondence, the kidnappers had replied to each ad in hours. But now days passed without a word. Charley's parents had to believe that the criminals had carried out their repeated threats to kill the boy. By Sunday, July 12, the third day of silence, the police were sufficiently alarmed to feel a change in tactics was necessary. The personal they prepared followed the abductors' instructions to the letter: "Ros I is got it and be wilin to pay it."

Whatever hope Christian and Sarah Ross had for the return of their son began to vanish as no word was received from the kidnappers. Neither would admit it to the other but both were in reality mourning their son. But then, once again, their hopes were renewed by the receipt of note #5.

This time Ross was ordered: "have the $20,000 in demonination not exceeding 'tens' have yu money were yu can git it any moment wen cal for…" To convince him that he would indeed have Charley at home "in 5 ours after we receive the mony and find it correct," they argued: "After we gets the mony we has no further use for the child, and it is to our interest then to restor him home unharmed, so that others will rely on our word."

The police and citizen's committee pounced on the writers' stated self-interest in returning the boy unharmed once they had the ransom. Although they had not taken the threats to Charley's life seriously, they now took in earnest the criminals' expressed intent to build a kidnapping business. It proved that payment of the ransom would guarantee other children would be kidnapped.

Clearly this could not be allowed. The committee increased the pressure on Ross, knowing how desperately he wanted to buy back his son. At home he had to face the accusation of Charley's empty bed, and the unspoken question, "When are you going to bring Charley home?" Tormented by his sense of inadequacy as a father, he could only repeat the reassurances impressed upon him at his meetings with the authorities; but they sounded hollow to him, and he knew Sarah had no faith in them.

For his wife there was no conflict, no wavering, no indecision. No matter what the cost, or what rules were broken, no matter what anyone thought, she wanted her son, quickly. She listened dutifully to her husband's explanations of strategy and tactics, but they had no effect on her. Of course, she was not asked to the meetings. That was for the men. A good wife of her time and position could not quarrel with the decisions of her husband. She had promised. She kept her promise. The only signs of her disobedience were her dreadful misery and her growing illness.

Now that he knew the terms, Ross was at a crucial turning point. The money was not a problem any longer. He could have borrowed it from his wife's family. Indeed, a complete stranger had offered to give it to him. But he was still a prisoner of his upper-middle-class upbringing, still committed to belonging.

Even so, the committee did not trust him not to deal with the kidnappers.

He had to consent to a twenty-four hour tail by plainclothesmen, the new plan to entrap the criminals, although he'd been warned "any fals act on yu part seals the fate of yu child and closes any further bisniss with us." His next ad was the ultimate false act. "Ros. It is redy. You have my word for it." But nobody ever came for the supposedly ready $20,000.

During the two weeks Charley had been absent, the five anonymous letters had been mailed from the Philadelphia main post office,.despite a police watch. But following a story in the *Philadelphia Inquirer* that the post office was under surveillance, the police demanded a news blackout. Some papers attacked this attempt "to muzzle the free press," adding nasty comments about police ineffectiveness, bungling, and stupidity.

As a result of the police and press name-calling, a valuable lead was lost. The sixth ransom letter was mailed at a street post office box in Philadelphia. This communication was an apology. The reason the ransom had not been called for was: "we had to go a bit out in the country an the blasted old orse give out so we could not get back in time." They swore, "may our blasted sols be eternaly damed if we do not keep our word." They warned again not to let the detectives know they were coming for the money, which was to be put in a "smal strong ruf box" and made available at a minute's notice.

Message #6 revealed a thoughtful analysis of the social forces involved in the affair. "let yu friends advise yu," the writer pleads, "not the detectives they study their own interest and the interest of society yu have a duty to perform to yourself that stands paramount to all else in the world…"

The letter was received on Thursday, July 16. It set Saturday the 20th as the day the abductors would be ready to exchange boy for money. The police assumed that the criminals were not only simpleminded, but that they would not carry out their threat to destroy the child. They staked out the Ross house, planning to trail whoever came for the money, and in one swoop arrest criminals and recover Charley.

From Friday night until Sunday morning Sarah and Christian Ross waited for a knock on their door. Keeping vigil with them, in hiding places, were detectives. Hour after hour passed in tense, expectant silence. But no messenger came.

It turned out that the kidnappers had not kept the rendezvous because they had been reading the newspapers.

They accused Ross of double dealing: "Ros: we be at a loss to understand yu a week ago yu sed yu had the amont an was wilin to pay it the editorials seme to speak as if the mony was yet to be contributed befor yu could pay it." They recognized the mistake they had made in assuming he was as affluent as the circumstances of his life indicated. But there was no turning back. "we thought yu were better fixt for money or we would never took yu child but since we have him we shal cary out our plan with him." Despite all, they were still willing to deal, but "dont yu state in personals that yu have the mony until yu have it naled up in the box an redy to give wen caled for."

In response to the public outcry for action the police made an arrest. The suspect, named Wooster, was a glib, fast-talking swindler with a long record. The evidence against him was a similarity between his penmanship and that of the ransom notes. The kidnappers took time to let it be known that Wooster was innocent. Wooster agreed with them. He defended himself by maintaining that there were easier ways of making a stake than stealing kids. After a week, during which the press tried him and found him guilty at first, then absolved him, Wooster was reluctantly released by the police.

Interviewed by the *New York Herald* when he was freed, Wooster editorialized about the case from the point of view of a professional criminal. He was convinced that the boy would not be returned unless the ransom was paid — the whole $20,000.

Why? "What would you reckon as fair compensation for giving up home and being in exile for the rest of your life?" he reasoned. "The publicity had made Philadelphia uninhabitable for the abductors." Is $20,000 too much when you are debarred from such rich, gullible cities as Philadelphia, guarded by such an idiotic police force? This professional estimate of police inadequacy from the other side of the law was agreed with by many law-abiding citizens.

Press criticism of the police mounted as some of the reporters began to do their own detecting. They found many loopholes in the nets the police had cast, found other promising leads the police had overlooked, but nothing came of them. Philadelphia's Mayor Stokeley's response to press urging that the city offer a reward for the return of the child was to reject it. He compared the kidnapping to stealing property. "When goods are stolen I don't wish them returned so much as I wish those who stole them brought to justice," he declared. The issue was never more bluntly stated. He went further. "If anyone on the force turns up stolen goods without bringing the thief to prison, the officer will be discharged."

Mayor Stokeley's attitude seems outrageous today. But in the America of that day, when the priority of property rights over human rights was largely unchallenged, it was very reasonable. The Mayor was only voicing the belief of his propertied constituency. It was appalling to Christian Ross that his son was thought of as "stolen goods," but he was a member of that constituency, and he could not yet free himself.

Of course, the kidnappers read the Mayor's

pronouncement. They read as well an interview with Christian Ross in which he said: "I place no confidence in these men and shall not do as they request." And the reverse: "Thus far I have no fears for the child's safety. All the letters assure me the child is safe and in good health." And, reversing himself again, "My greatest apprehension is that, finding they do not get the money, the child may suffer for it."

Not my child, but "the child." Odd for a father to refer to his son in such a manner. How, after pledging to negotiate and accept their terms, could he say he never had any intention of dealing with them? Does his contradictory statement, widely reprinted, make sense? If he has no confidence in the men, why does he accept their statement that the boy is safe? And if his non-confidence in their threats is true, why then does he have apprehensions for the boy's life if the money is not paid?

Obviously, the meeting between authority and Ross in which this letter was composed reflects Ross' real feeling only in part. No one knows how much he struggled against the committee. Regardless of what he felt, his statement told the kidnappers they would return the boy when they finally realized that the ransom would never be paid.

It may be that Ross was led to agree to defy the criminals because on July 22, the next day, handbills were distributed throughout the city offering:

$20,000 REWARD FOR THE KIDNAPPERS

The money had been contributed by bankers and other men of means meeting with Mayor Stokeley. It was to be paid "for the arrest and conviction of the abductors of CHARLES BREWSTER ROSS... and the restoration of the child to his parents." In that order. The offer was accompanied by a description of the two men and the boy. Somehow, inexplicably, it neglected to mention the older man's grotesque "monkey nose."

The nationally circulated reward offer produced a spate of Charley Rosses and arrests all over the country. But it left the mystery still unsolved.

Evidently convinced that the kidnappers were imbeciles and had not read Ross' widely printed refusal to negotiate, the authorities bought another personal ad. It said: "Money is ready. How shall I know your agent?"

Logically there was no earthly reason to expect any response to this obviously phony communication. Yet there was a logic to the answer mailed in Camden, New Jersey.

The writer noted the conflict between Ross' statement of no confidence and the "money is ready" ad. "nevertheless we wil act upon yu promise as if it was made by an angle." This was because: "from the nature of this bisiness it is to be presumed neither can have implicit confidence." It reiterated that once they had the ransom they would have no fur-

A Pinkerton poster announcing a reward for Charley's return.

ther use for Charley and would return him. And it added a postscript about identifying their agent. "we wil send prof with him so yu can no him when he comes."

Ross' personal on July 22 agreed to comply in every particular. It was answered by a strange note on July 24, which announced a week's delay because "our creed is such it forbids us to do any bisiness of this kind only at a certain quarter of the moon."

This is the only known instance of criminals being astrologically guided. Perhaps the police would have been more successful if they had looked to the zodiac for leadership.

The writer regretted the postponement: "this delay may be a great sorce of torture to yu but it cannot be avoided." They must have been reading Ross' mind when they jeered at the reward offer, "not one cent for ransom but millions for conviction," a paraphrase of the historical statement defying the Barbary pirates: "Millions for defense but not one cent for tribute." It is extremely unlikely that the bereaved parents could find a satisfactory answer to the question: "Why do they not pay their mony to have yours restored first an then offer a reward for our conviction?"

The Ross family continued to be deluged with advice, suggestions, correspondence. Their home was invaded by crackpots of all kinds, publicity seekers; religious fanatics; mediums with clues from the other world; con men hoping to latch on to a fast buck; inquiring reporters in various disguises; and well-intentioned sympathizers with offers of money. The sensation-seeking press, lacking scoops, made them up. In this heyday of yellow journalism, any rumor, innuendo, character assassination was fit to print. Headlined were anonymous letters which cast suspicion on Mr. and Mrs. Ross and even Walter as accomplices in the crime. The press pointed to Ross' need of money, suggested that Charley was buried on the Ross property, talked of skeletons in the family closet which caused Ross to spirit the boy away, charged that the anonymous letters were written by Ross himself. Ultimately Ross brought a libel suit against the *Philadelphia Eagle* which called the kidnapping a fraud. The paper was fined. But the libels didn't cease.

When the moon turned to the favorable phase desired by the kidnappers, on July 28, they wrote Ross to have the money ready by the 30th. More detectives were added to the detail concealed in and around the Ross home, prepared for the visitor on the 30th.

On the 30th no visitor came. Instead there arrived a foolproof scheme to avoid entrapment. It ordered Ross to journey by train that very afternoon to New York City and thence to Albany. Somewhere along this route he would be given a signal, a bell and white flag by day, a torch and flag by night. He was told to stand on the rear platforms of the trains. When he saw the signal, he was to throw out a valise with the ransom. But if the train stopped and the signaler was arrested: "you child's fate is sealed." And finally if contact had not been made when he reached Albany, he would find a letter in the Albany post office directing him where to continue his journey.

This letter was different from all the others. There was no attempt to negotiate, or to persuade, or to point out the mistakes Ross was making. It was an ultimatum.

Most ominous to Ross was the final sentence: "this letter ends all things in regard to the restoration of yu child."

Another meeting decided that Ross was to go on the journey as directed, except that he would be accompanied by his nephew and a plainclothesman, and instead of the money, the valise would contain a letter. It was composed by the committee, signed by Ross, and it insisted, "I cannot throw away twenty thousand dollars on the wild plan you suggested." It proposed a simultaneous exchange — money for boy.

Valise in hand, Ross stood on the rear platforms of the train from Philadelphia to New York, his eyes straining for the signal that might come any place along the way. There was none. The detective trailed him through Grand Central Station in New York to the rear platform post on the Albany train. No torch lit up the gathering darkness. Nor was there the promised letter in the Albany post office. Ross stayed over in Albany. Perhaps the letter had been delayed. But no letter arrived.

What had gone wrong? What had prevented the criminals from going through with their plan? Had they changed their minds? The explanation was received at Ross' place of business during his absence. On July 30th newspaper extras proclaimed that Charley Ross had been found in the town of Hamburg, seventy-five miles from Philadelphia, and that Ross had gone there to claim his boy.

Accordingly the kidnappers had concluded Ross was still not convinced that only they had Charley, and only they could return him. Naturally, they'd called off their agent. They were now giving him a last chance. His intentions should be made known in a personal addressed to John.

On August 2, thirty-two days after the search for Charley had begun, Ross advertised, "Your directions were followed. You did not keep faith. Point out some sure and less public way of communicating either by letter or person."

In the next day's letter the criminals acknowledged their mistake. They told Ross to have the money in the box, ready in his store. They went so far as to promise, "if we lose our money through our agent yu get yu child just as if we got every dollar."

Taking the criminals' continuance of negotiations as a sign of their weakness, the authorities took a hard line. Ross answered, "Propositions are impossible. Action must be simultaneous." On August 4th the criminals wrote: "We shal not communicate with yu any more unles yu want to redeem yu child on our terms." They left one way out for Ross. "if you have anything to say to us it must be through the personals of the *New York Herald.*"

Clearly they were matching the hard line of the police. The police got even tougher. They completely ignored the note for the next three weeks. During this time both sides clung to their immovable positions. Contact was broken.

The action of the drama shifted to New York in September, when a convicted horse thief and burglar, Gil Mosher, accused his fifty-two-year-old brother, William, of being the kidnapper. He told New York Police Superintendent George Walling that his brother Bill had once proposed they kidnap one of Commodore Vanderbilt's grandchildren with a plan identical to the Ross abduction. He went on to implicate Bill's partner, a younger man, Joe Douglas, and as a clincher he produced examples of Bill's handwriting which the police decided were similar to that of the ransom notes.

From this point on, the police were convinced that Bill Mosher and Joe Douglas were the men they were looking for, though Gil's credibility as a witness was less than solid. They knew he wanted to revenge himself on his brother for having cheated him out of the proceeds of a robbery, and that he would sell his mother for the reward or any part of it. Yet his information was as close as they had come to any break in the case.

As soon as Mosher was accused, a New York detective who had once arrested Bill Mosher remembered that his prisoner had a deformed nose, which made him fit little Walter Ross' description, "the man with the monkey nose."

Now a national search for Bill Mosher and Joe Douglas was launched. And because the New York police knew Bill was a devoted husband and father who could be expected to be in touch with his family, a hunt was ordered for his wife, Martha, and her four children. It should have been easier to locate Martha and her kids than the wanted men, but it wasn't.

In his eagerness for the reward, Gil gave the police another lead. He pointed them at Martha's brother, William Westervelt, a former policeman discharged from the force for covering up a gambling ring, part-time horsecar conductor, and bosom buddy of Bill Mosher. Westervelt was picked up and held till little Walter Ross could be brought from Philadelphia to take a look at him. The boy was certain that he was not one of the men who had taken him and Charley for a ride.

Usually when a suspect of less than blameless character is cleared, he tends to put as much distance between himself and the police as possible. Not Westervelt. He had some fish he wanted New York's finest to fry for him.

A drawing depicting the kidnapping of Charley Ross.

Of all the extraordinary circumstances in this case, the police connection with Westervelt was to prove the most bizarre. From moment to moment he changed from stool pigeon to his brother-in-law's keeper, and back again. During the months the New York police believed they were manipulating him, he was manipulating the police. When he was caught in a lie, or his double dealing was exposed, Westervelt always admitted it, always had a persuasive explanation.

The relationship with Westervelt, during which the trail got alternately hot and cold, was kept top secret. Christian Ross had no part in it. It was all out of his hands. All he was allowed to do was take instructions, and check out the increasing number of Charley Rosses that kept being found after a group of eminent Philadelphians hired the Pinkertons, America's most famous eyes. These sleuths distributed millions of circulars which turned up Charleys in almost every state, and Canada and Cuba.

When the New York police saw fit they reported their progress to the Philadelphia police, who in their turn reported to Ross what they thought he should know. It may be that the less he was told about the frustrating twists and turns the New York inquiry took at Westervelt's direction, the better off he was.

The head man in New York, Police Superintendent George Walling, dealt personally with Westervelt — the closest they had come to the kidnappers. Unlike the ordinary informer who wants cash for his wares, Westervelt wanted to be paid in services. In return for letting Walling know when he next heard from Mosher, he wanted the superintendent to get him full-time employment from the horsecar company, and/or reinstatement in the police department. His third condition was that his cooperation with the police remain secret. Walling agreed to everything.

When Walling was getting nowhere with the horsecar owners or the police board, Westervelt put on some pressure. It took an emotional turn. He could not in all decency finger his brother-in-law because it would be so terrible for his poor innocent sister and her little ones. Walling was very understanding. Blood, he agreed, was much thicker than water. It would be inhuman to expect Westervelt to betray Mosher. All Westervelt need do was lead him to Douglas. Westervelt was vastly relieved by the Superintendent's display of compassion.

Who was kidding whom? If the policeman thought the informer was too dumb to realize that Douglas would lead to Mosher, he was mistaken. In this game of wits he was outmatched. Walling was to learn that his trickiness was to work against him.

The informer insisted that though he was in his brother-in-law's confidence, he had never heard him mention a word about kidnapping Charley Ross or anyone else. He also swore from his knowledge of Mosher that it was impossible for him to steal a child. Having thus told the police what they did not want to hear, Westervelt smoothly reversed himself. He managed to remember that in June, only weeks before Charley was stolen, Bill had proudly shown him a horse and buggy he had just bought. Walling dug out a composite drawing of the kidnap buggy, made from the description of witnesses. Westervelt studied it carefully and said that, except for some minor details, it mirrored the one Mosher had bought.

Splendid. Here was more evidence against Mosher. Obviously, Westervelt was the key to the case. But a very slippery key. At their next meeting, Westervelt was indignant because he had been dragged from his job to headquarters, and Walling was in a fury. The Superintendent had ordered Westervelt's arrest because he'd learned the informer had known all along where Martha Mosher was living. Why had he withheld this important information? Westervelt blandly reminded Walling that he had agreed only to help capture Douglas, not his sister's husband.

Walling was stuck. He was party to the blood-is-thicker-than-water deal. If he were going to get any further help from Westervelt, he had to do it Westervelt's way. He cooled down and amity was restored. Westervelt gave evidence of his good intentions by coming up with a list of saloons where Mosher and Douglas hung out. And to prove his support of the treaty, Walling arranged a reinstatement interview with the police board for the informer.

In Philadelphia, the strategy committee continued to meet and ponder Walling's progress reports, but without Christian Ross. The unremitting strain of the passing months had proved too much for him. He had broken down physically and mentally, and was confined to his bed. Sarah Ross' brothers, Henry and Joseph Lewis, took over the family's end of the case. These strong-minded businessmen at first cooperated with the Philadelphia committee, then, as they became disgusted with the self-righteous attitude of their peers, struck out on their own.

On September 25th, the kidnappers wrote:

"if yu compel us to put him to death yu shall receive a letter in 24 ours after where yu will find his body..."

The Lewises took this seriously and replied accepting their terms. And they meant it. This did not sit well with the authorities who had not deviated from their original attitude. The Lewises were determined to do it their way. They were not impressed by the arguments that had overwhelmed Ross. Not even the optimistic reports from Walling could budge them.

The truth of the matter was that Walling's optimism rested on a shifty foundation. All he had to go on was Westervelt, but he didn't really have him. A bartender reported several recent visits to his saloon of the two suspects during which they huddled with Westervelt. When Walling confronted his ally with this evidence of complicity, the informer had a glib explanation. The meetings were accidental and so brief that he hadn't an opportunity to call the police. But he gave his word that if he ran into them again, he'd notify Walling immediately. What could Walling do?

The Lewis brothers received their final, detailed, instructions from the kidnappers on October 31. The $20,000 in small bills was to be taken to New York. The bearer should advertise what hotel he was stopping at. He should remain there until their agent came for the money. Within hours after the ransom was paid, Charley would be released with an identifying label on his back.

Though the Lewises were determined to go through with the transaction despite the committee's disapproval, they were not yet ready to break completely with it. They agreed reluctantly to try to bargain further with the kidnappers who refused to budge from their position. It took almost three weeks before they declared their independence from the committee, and went to New York with the ransom. Unfortunately, as it turned out, they compromised their freedom by informing the authorities of the coming transaction.

The Lewises, with a valise crammed with $20,000 in unmarked small bills, registered at the Fifth Avenue Hotel in New York on the night of November 17th. They duly communicated their whereabouts to the kidnappers as ordered. They remained in their room all day and night of the 18th. No emissary came to collect the ransom. Deeply disappointed and convinced that the authorities were right — you could not deal honestly with criminals — they checked out and took themselves back to Philadelphia. What they did not know was that Philadelphia had informed New York, and that Walling had infiltrated the hotel with dozens of detectives. So much for honest dealing.

Once again in sync with the committee, the Lewis family put an ad in the *New York Herald* on the 19th of November:

> We have performed our part. You have broken faith. We will have no more trifling. Action must now be taken simultaneous.

Strong words, but shouted into a void. They waited for a reply. On the basis of previous experience an answer would be forthcoming. There was no immediate reply. There was never to be a reply.

Less than a month later Society caught up with Mosher and Douglas on Long Island where they tripped the burglar alarm in the Van Brunt summer home. The newspapers, the police, and the public agreed unanimously that double justice had been done. When the Van Brunts and their hired hands blasted the housebreakers, they had, though inadvertently, also punished the kidnappers of Charley Ross. There was no one except Mosher's grief-stricken widow who doubted that Mosher had stolen Charley. Euphoric with relief that the case had been solved, the nation disregarded a fundamental tenet of American justice, that guilt must be proven beyond a reasonable doubt. Mosher and Douglas never had their day in court before a jury of their peers. No one was ever to hear their defense.

With the kidnappers out of the way, all that remained was to find Charley. At first the police reasoned that whoever was keeping the boy would hasten to let him go, in fear of the same fate that Mosher and his partner had met. Charley would be home by Christmas, they predicted. But that didn't happen. And the New Year came, but it was not a very happy occasion for the police because Charley was still missing, and the press and public had begun to turn against them.

It had begun to dawn on the man and woman in the street that the police achievement thus far was zero. All their efforts, schemes and stratagems to find the kidnappers had been useless. If it hadn't been for vigilant citizens, Mosher and Douglas would still be alive. Unless Charley was found right quick police heads ought to roll.

Walling, who had been busy taking unjustified bows for the death of the suspects, felt the pressure most keenly. He came down as hard as he could on Westervelt who swore he had no knowledge about where the boy was. Walling had to come up with something to divert criticism from himself, and he came up with Westervelt.

On the pretext that Christian Ross wanted to talk to him, Walling got Westervelt to go to Philadelphia. There were police waiting for him on his arrival. He was arrested and imprisoned, charged with abduction and conspiracy to abduct. Walling was to be the main witness against him.

Christian Ross got out of bed to visit Westervelt in jail. When he came out, he told reporters that Westervelt said, "Charley was alive when Mosher was killed." "As for myself," Ross added, "it would be a relief to know of his fate — whether dead or alive."

On August 30, 1875, Westervelt took his place in the dock and pleaded "Not guilty" to all the charges. The prosecution, recognizing it had not the slightest circumstantial case of abduction, concentrated on Westervelt's complicity with Mosher and Douglas. The dangerous game he had played with Walling now became damning evidence against him when the Superintendent testified. The principal issue in the case was the District Attorney's contention that Westervelt had consistently misled the police and shielded the kidnappers, in order to get a share of the ransom money.

In opposition, the defense argued that

Walling was using Westervelt as a scapegoat to cover up his ineptness. Westervelt was on the stand for four days, insisting that he had cooperated with the police. The defense rested its case after a final question:

"William Westervelt, can you now furnish, or could you at any time have furnished any clue to the abduction of the child, Charles Brewster Ross?"

"No. I wish to God I could," the defendant answered.

The jury's inability to agree on a verdict caused an adjournment for a weekend. When they returned, the foreman announced they had found Westervelt innocent of abduction, but guilty of conspiracy to abduct, to extort money, and to deprive Charley of his liberty.

On October 9, 1875, Judge Elcock gave Westervelt the maximum sentence allowed by law — seven years of solitary confinement at hard labor. Ross dragged himself down to the prison and promised to help Westervelt get a pardon if he had any information about Charley, alive or dead. Westervelt swore that he knew nothing.

In January, 1881, model prisoner William Westervelt, with a year off for good behavior, was released from prison. He still maintained his innocence, and pledged he would devote himself to finding Charley. But nothing further was ever heard from him.

The hunt for Charley Ross went on during the following decades. More supposed Charleys kept turning up, and Christian Ross continued to check them out, unwilling to leave any possibility uninvestigated. His quest for his son ended only with his death in 1897.

Sarah Ross continued the search into the twentieth century when her little boy would have grown into a middle-aged man. As she grew too feeble to travel, she sent her brothers to talk to 40-year-olds who claimed they were Charley.

In 1943, Charley's big brother Walter, a retired stockbroker, reported that the parade of claimants was still continuing. Over the years more than 5,000 boys and men had identified themselves as Charley Ross. A century after the four-year-old was stolen, an item occasionally appears in the press about someone who says he is a great-grandson of Charley Ross. But the question of what happened to the real Charley Ross remains unanswered.

THE VANISHING BONES

Although it is no longer the world's tallest man-made structure, the Empire State Building, which rises a quarter of a mile above Fifth Avenue and 34th Street in New York City, continues to attract millions of visitors to the observatory on the 102nd floor. The view on a clear day is spectacular. You can see fifty miles in every direction except south, where the twin peaks of the World Trade Center loom up in the way at the tip of Manhattan.

Since it was topped out in 1931, the skyscraper has withstood stresses and strains the architects could not have anticipated. It has, for example, been struck by airplanes, human flies have tried to walk up its sides, kids have tried to spit down from its dizzying heights, and so on. Less traumatic has been its use as a trysting place by innumerable romantically inclined couples.

By far the most famous pair ever to occupy the tower top were a lovesick monster gorilla, ten basketball centers high, King Kong — from the movie of the same name — and the beautiful woman-sized object of his unrequited affection, played by Fay Wray. The world will long remember the tragic end of that star-crossed romance: royal Kong nobly protecting Fay while he is being shot down from the summit by an armada of U.S. Air Force fighters. In the remake of the King Kong film, the site for Kong's last stand is the twin Trade towers.

To be sure, this sort of thing is not an everyday occurrence on the Empire State. Most if not all dating pairs are likely to be better assorted, somewhat less noticeable. Into this stuffy category you would have put the attractive housewife-type and the prosperous businessman-type who had their heads together in a corner of the observatory on the afternoon of June 27, 1973. That's supposing you noticed them at all.

There was no reason to look again, except if you were bemused by their being more mature than most daters — she in her forties, he some twenty years older. But if you didn't mind your own business, and peered more closely, you'd have seen that she kept a wary eye on anyone who came near, then suddenly, terrified, bolted for the elevator. Her companion, caught flatfooted, gave chase, but in vain.

Well, there's nothing so extraordinary about a couple quarreling and breaking up, temporarily or permanently. It happens often in real life. In movie life it is standard operating procedure.

As it happens, this particular scene would not be acceptable to filmmakers, because it led to no happy ending — nor to any ending at all.

Besides it would be terribly difficult to make the story believable if you stuck to the facts like:

Tycoon turns private eye at sixty to find persons missing a half-million years before he was born; involved in his quest are relics which are simultaneously worthless and beyond price. Great powers are at loggerheads. The U.S. Marines come to the rescue and have to be rescued. Dead men, women, and children tell tales. Scholars stake reputations on dragon bones.

The characters are real enough; it's the complications they get into that seem to go beyond belief. Take the man on the top of the Empire State. There was nothing mysterious about him until he took it upon himself to solve the mystery. His name was and is Christopher G. Janus, Chicago stockbroker, self-made millionaire, philanthropist — the money behind a foundation devoted to international exchange.

Mr. Janus was a late entrant into the plot.

Christopher Janus, holding the photograph given to him
by the "mystery woman."

He was on a cultural exchange mission to the People's Republic of China, in the spring of 1973 when, as he was to report, a high government official took him away from a reception and said:

"Help us find Peking Man. If you can return Peking Man to us, you will be a hero to the Chinese people."

If he became a hero to 800,000,000 Chinese, Mr. Janus reasoned, it would doubtlessly help better relations between China and the U.S.A. So Mr. Janus blithely said he would be glad to oblige. Since he had never heard of the missing man, he hadn't the remotest notion of what he was getting himself into.

Mr. Janus soon learned that his mission was not the kind of thing a police missing persons bureau could help him with. Just for starters Peking Man had vanished twice — the first time in 500,000 B.C., the second, after he had reappeared and been around for fifteen years, in 1941. Another unique aspect of his disappearance both times is that his entire family — some forty persons of both sexes and various ages — went with him.

Some of Mr. Janus' information came from scholarly journals, some from the press. His most authoritative source was the amateur detective who had headed up the investigation for more than thirty years, Dr. Harry L. Shapiro. An eminent scientist, Chairman of the Department of Anthropology at the American Museum of Natural History, Dr. Shapiro had not abandoned hope that Peking Man would and could be located.

Shapiro's optimism could not have sprung from any new, more promising leads than all previous clues. If he refused to be dismayed, it must have been because, impossible as the solution to the '41 disappearance seemed, it was a snap compared to the earlier one. This time they knew they were looking for Peking Man. The investigators in the 1920's didn't know he was missing, didn't even know that he had ever existed.

How can you possibly find someone whose existence is unknown? Well, first you have to believe in dragon bones. Where do you go for them? To the drugstore. In pre-revolutionary China they were sold for a few yen without a doctor's prescription. Ground to a powder, and taken as directed by your neighborhood pharmacist, they were considered a cure for anything and everything that ailed you.

The trail that led to the discovery of Peking Man began in Chou Kou Tien drugstore some thirty miles from Peking. The scientists who were browsing along the dragon bone counter stumbled upon a couple of them that seemed different from the everyday assortment. All the others were the petrified remains of pre-historic beasts. This pair of fossils stunned the browsers. They resembled, or seemed to resemble, human teeth.

They were no more prepared for this than Columbus was to find the new world sticking up out of the ocean. Science had never considered the possibility that a branch of the human family tree had sprouted in China. Concealing their excitement, so as not to raise the price, the scientists bought the molars, for intensive laboratory study.

Meanwhile, the wholesaler who supplied bones to the drugstore was tracked down, and he led to his source of supply — a mound known to the local residents as Chicken Bone Hill. The surrounding area was a mine of fossilized remains of sabre-toothed tigers and other extinct animals. Interesting specimens but disappointing. It took a lot of digging back through time before they found what they were looking for — proof that creatures like humans had lived out their lives in this part of the world ages ago.

There wasn't much to go on at first, altogether three molars. Hardly enough for a distinguished scientist to risk his career and reputation on. Nevertheless, Dr. Davidson Black, head of Peking Union Medical College, under whose auspices the dig was being conducted, stuck his neck out and gained scientific immortality. He could just as easily have achieved oblivion for the uncompromisingly blunt, revolutionary announcement he made in 1927:

"The actual presence of early man in Eastern Asia is no longer a matter of conjecture."

Strong words for a scientist, especially for one who had no formal training in the required special fields of archaeology, paleontology, geology. Black had an M.D. from a Canadian university. His reputation was based upon his unquestionable contributions as an anatomist. The kindest thing the specialists could find to say about him was that as an amateur he didn't know what he was doing, and like so many well-meaning novices he had an obsession about the origin of the human species.

It was certainly true that Black was a man with a twelve-year-old obsession. In 1914, he had made a trip to England to study with the preeminent anatomist Professor Elliot Smith. Black became fascinated by a project Smith was working on — restoring the head of a prehistoric man out of fossil fragments that had been unearthed in Piltdown, England, three years earlier.

The influence Piltdown Man had on young Dr. Black can be compared to that a great athlete has on an adolescent. But most adolescents give up their dreams of being Tom Seaver or Billie Jean King. Black never gave up his of finding the missing link in the human chain.

If Black had known the truth about Piltdown Man, whose discovery had revolutionized science, he would not have been so inspired, and Peking Man would never have been discovered. At the very least our common ancestor's reentrance would have been postponed indefinitely without Black. For

Piltdown Man was a phony — the supposedly ancient skull fragments were those of modern man, aged as some unscrupulous antique dealers add years to their wares. And the bits of his jaw were those of an ape.

But Black's illusion was never to be dissipated. Piltdown Man remained enthroned in science during his lifetime. Black died in 1934, and the fraud was discovered by a pair of British scientists, who had kept restudying the bone pieces, in 1955.

Ironically, Black's establishment critics kept comparing his treasured molars with Piltdown's skull and jaw bones, much to Black's disadvantage. It wasn't until 1929 that Peking Man came close to matching Piltdown's eminence.

It was fitting that crowning evidence of Peking Man's existence, a sizeable hunk of his skull, was found by a Chinese member of Black's staff — Dr. W.C. Pei. Vindication, but not enough for Black and his colleagues. They continued to scrape and sift back through geologic time, stopping only occasionally when they were caught in the line of fire between battling Chinese warlords.

By the time the Japanese occupation of China in 1937 had put a permanent halt to the excavation, they had bit by bit accumulated a priceless scientific treasure — by far the largest collection of proofs to the existence of a vanished branch of the human family tree. Previous to this time, the evolutionary descent, or ascent of man, depended upon the scanty fragmented remains of single individuals. These bones had been left by a whole tribe, forty creatures enough akin to us to know the uses of fire.

Davidson Black's abundant proof that *Sinanthropus pekinesis* (Chinese man from Peking) was a distant relative of modern *Homo sapiens* (Wise man) made a big impression on the scientific community.

The men who manned Peking Medical College's Cenozoic Research Laboratory labeled, photographed, and made casts of every precious bit of their treasure. No mortal remains were ever so honored, so artfully tended, so watched over.

Yet despite all the attention given him, despite the fact that his guardians knew that he was in danger and had done everything to protect him, he had disappeared. By the time Mr. Janus took it upon himself to find him, Peking Man had long been out of the eye of the press, and everybody had given him up, with the single exception of Dr. Shapiro.

The scientist recognized that the stockbroker's optimism more than matched his own, though it came from a different lifestyle. Janus' confidence that the mystery could be solved was based upon his conviction that money — with which he was amply supplied — could work miracles; and it was precisely a miracle that was required in this case.

It's an understatement to say the circumstances were mind-boggling. The remnants of Peking Man had last been seen when they were packed away in two boxes by their laboratory custodians, back in late November, 1941. This was the scientists' last desperate attempt to remove them from jeopardy by getting them out of the country. Again and again during the preceding year as war threatened, the scientists had tried to have the bones removed to the United States for safekeeping.

There were great difficulties in the way. All the research was funded by the Rockefeller Foundation and based on agreement with China that the fossils were to remain in their native land. Consequently, any move to take the precious bones out of China would be a violation of the agreement, and subject them to confiscation by customs. Under the chaotic conditions that existed, the scholars didn't dare risk letting Peking Man fall into bureaucratic hands.

One way to keep the find free from molestation was to have it sent out in a diplomatic pouch. Urgent pleas for such a safe conduct were made to the U.S. Ambassador, Nelson Johnson, but he understandably had other priorities.

There was one final way out for the fossils. A detachment of U.S. Marines were preparing to ship out for the Philippines, and it was arranged the boxes would go with them.

The boxes were sent care of Pharmacist's Mate Herman Davis at Camp Holcomb, in

A drawing of the artist's conception of the Peking Man.

Chingwantao. Davis and his buddies were already packed to leave, and he put the two boxes, which were almost identical with Marine footlockers, along with his own stuff where he could keep a watchful eye on them. Neither Davis, nor the seventeen others in the medical unit, nor the fossil footlockers ever reached the Philippines. It wouldn't have mattered much if they had, because the next day Japanese warplanes bombed Pearl Harbor, and not long after, the Philippines were captured.

Davis and his men found themselves prisoners of war in a Tientsin camp. It took a while before the Japanese got around to sending the prisoners their belongings from Camp Holcomb. And when Davis got his, he discovered his personal baggage had been looted, and the two footlockers he had guarded had not arrived. There was nothing he could do about it.

Was Peking Man a casualty of World War II? Had the enemy soldiers who'd scavenged through the Marines' possessions thrown the old bones away? They stole only what was valuable, or useful. You couldn't expect a Japanese infantryman to know the scientific value of the contents of the boxes, could you? Well, no, and yes.

Even before the outbreak of hostilities between the United States and Japan, Japanese scientists had shown an acquisitive interest in Peking Man, proud evidence that our species was born in Asia. They were able through the Japanese military presence in China to keep a close watch on the work going on at Peking Medical College, but couldn't interfere with it because correct diplomatic relations had to be maintained with the United States. But after December 7th, no holds were barred. The Imperial High Command gave the bones top priority as a prize of war. It seems impossible that their disciplined troops would discard the fossils the officers were searching for. And if they had been found at Camp Holcomb or along the route to the prison, they might well have been sent to Tokyo.

All the questions about the vanished bones had to remain unanswered during the next four years of bloody warfare. Three months after the original, primitive atom bombs turned Hiroshima and Nagasaki back to the Stone Age, the *New York Times* came up with a solution to the mystery:

SAVE PEKING MAN RELICS

read a November 20, 1945, headline. The story filed by the *Times* man in Tokyo reported that the fossils had been found among other war loot at Tokyo Imperial University. Two weeks later the discovery was confirmed by *Newsweek* magazine's correspondent in Shanghai:

PEKING MAN IS SAFE

There was jubilation in the halls of the Museum of Natural History. And indeed fossils from the dig at Chou Kouo Tien, which had been taken by the Japanese from the College laboratory, were found in Tokyo. But they were the remains of the animals Peking Man had hunted, and the stone tools he had used. Of the body he had inhabited, there was no trace.

The postwar search in Japan, then occupied by the American military, got nowhere. The logical place to look was China, and approaches were made to the U.S. State Department for assistance. But the State Department was not responsive. Even if the diplomats had been, the civil war that broke out in China after the Japanese had surrendered effectively prevented any investigation.

Through the years, Dr. Shapiro and his colleagues kept following up any leads no matter how slight. One story that astounded them was that Peking Man had been stolen by Americans and was in the possession of Dr. Shapiro. To this charge made by the Peoples' Republic of China, Dr. Shapiro gave the press a one word refutation:

"Nonsense."

What was in the Museum of Natural History was the sole remaining evidence that Peking Man had existed — casts, photographs, measurements of his skull and skeleton which had been removed from the laboratories and taken to the United States shortly before the outbread of war with Japan.

The American scientists would have liked to pick up the trail of the missing bones on the site where they had been lost. But during the period of the cold war with Mao Tse-tung's China, they hadn't any chance of being admitted to that land. With détente, there was some hope. The first indication that China was interested in a cooperative hunt with the Americans was their overture to Mr. Janus.

The method Janus proposed to Dr. Shapiro at their meeting was something no previous investigators had tried, or even thought of — buy a solution to the case. Offer a reward. A man of action, he no sooner said it than it was done. The press carried the announcement: $5,000 for the return or information leading to the return of Peking Man or any part of him.

Money produced a lot of talk. Mostly from people who didn't know what they were talking about but who were attracted by an easy $5,000. But there was one phone call, from a woman who wouldn't give her name, that rang some bells.

"I'm the widow of a Marine officer," she whispered. (Bell #1.)

"When he died," she continued, "he left me a footlocker with some skull and bone fragments he had gotten in China." (Bell #2.)

This was closer than any response to the reward offer had come to the facts of the case. Janus tried unsuccessfully to get more details. He invited the caller to lunch. Refused. Her voice was thin with fear. Of what, Janus could not make out. He proposed several other meeting places, at her convenience. She turned them all down. They were getting nowhere, until she suggested the top of the Empire State. How would he know her? He wouldn't. She'd know him.

Janus could not be at all sure that his blind date would show up. So he was more than pleasantly surprised when some minutes after he got off at the last elevator stop, an attractive woman in her forties gestured to him.

Janus followed her through the crowd of camera-wielding tourists into a corner of the observatory. He assured her that he had come alone, and she plunged hurriedly into her story.

Her husband had confessed to her before he died that the footlocker contained loot — valuable loot he had stolen from China and that she could get into serious trouble for possessing it. When he'd died, she'd opened the box and saw only the bones. She couldn't figure out what he had been talking about, and had kept the bones only as a memento of the departed. It wasn't until she read about the reward that she realized how valuable her legacy was.

In proof, she dug into her pocketbook and produced a photograph of the top layer of the contents of an old footlocker. Janus could recognize some skull and bone fragments, but had no idea whether they were those he was looking for. To his unscientific eye they looked human and fossilized, and his excitement grew. Where were they? When could they be seen? Before he made a deal, she must realize he had to have more than a photograph.

Fair enough? Yes. But before she answered any of his questions, he must agree to raise the reward offer. Accustomed as he was to negotiating matters involving six, seven, and more figures, Janus was nevertheless appalled to hear her evaluation of the fossils — $500,000,000. Of course, that could only be the asking price. He had just begun to bring it down, when a flash bulb popped somewhere near them, and the woman snatched the photo from him and vanished.

When Janus reported the aborted meeting to Dr. Shapiro, both agreed that the photograph might have been a fake. Nevertheless, they agreed that if it were possible the negotiations should be resumed. If Janus heard from the woman again, he should insist, tactfully of course, that before any money pass hands, the bones be examined by Dr. Shapiro, or some other scientist qualified to authenticate them.

Since Janus had no idea where the anonymous woman could be reached, all he could do was wait for her to surface. After a month had passed, time enough for her to have realized he'd not been trying to trap her on the tower, Janus tried to renew their brief ac-

The photograph of the Peking Man bones.

quaintance. His cryptic ad appeared where it was hard to miss, at the bottom of the first page of the *New York Times*, August 4, 1972:

PEKING MAN Emp. $1? Obs. mtg. Funds avail; no questions. Phone C.G.J. — Advt.

"I didn't really have much hope," Janus was to tell a *Times* reporter, "but sure enough it must have been a week later when I got a call from the woman.

"I asked her to send me a copy of the picture so I could have the fossils authenticated. She was reluctant. She said, 'How do I know someone will not authenticate them away from me?'

"Several times she spoke of the fossils being stolen property. Those were her words: 'stolen property.'"

Janus must have been very persuasive, because the mystery woman sent him a copy of the photograph that had excited him. With it in hand he hurried to Dr. Shapiro's office.

All that Dr. Shapiro would commit himself to was: "I have a strong suspicion that it's interesting. The skull has the shape of the Peking Man."

Dr. Shapiro's careful non-commitment was to be expected in the *modus operandi* of scientist-detectives. But another respected member of the scientific community was less circumspect.

Professor William Howells, a leading paleontologist, scrutinized the photograph and reported the skull, in his opinion, was definitely of the genus *Sinanthropus Pekinensis*. He went further to positively identify it as Skull fragment # XI.

What Janus had to contend with now was the widow's fear that she would wind up in jail for trying to dispose of stolen property. He took care of this by getting a widely publicized statement from the U.S. State Department. An Assistant Secretary for educational and cultural affairs pointed out to the widow through the press "the statute of limitations has expired," and thus, "the Federal Government would not be interested in prosecution."

He also appealed to the missing woman's patriotism:

"I hope you will be able to persuade the lady in question that she will be doing not only her duty but a genuine service to the United States, in coming forward with the fossils to make them available for return to the Peoples' Republic of China."

That should have done it, but it didn't. Only temporarily disappointed, Mr. Janus energetically followed up other leads. One came from a Chinese businessman in New York, who informed Janus:

"A friend of mine, a high official in the Chinese Nationalist Government in Taiwan, has the footlocker containing the bones."

The informant who insisted on anonymity quoted his official chum:

"He said there was a great deal of violence connected with getting these fossils and the family is terribly afraid." Janus was able to gather that the fear of violence could be assuaged for the right price. Well, this was a somewhat promising lead. It was known that when the Nationalist Chinese fled from the Communists, they naturally took with them anything of value they could carry. Why not Peking Man?

Janus took off for Taiwan. His ad in the Taiwanese press raised the ante for the return of the bones to $150,000. There was not even a crackpot response. This did not necessarily mean that the informant had been misinformed. But no one in that policed state would have dared to admit he had the fossils, and was willing to return them to the American who had promised them to the enemy Communist Chinese.

Janus hoped to overcome this problem by announcing to the Taiwanese reporters:

"I certainly don't want the bones to go to the Communists." This could not have helped him achieve his original intention of improving relations with the Peoples' Republic. From the diplomatic point of view, it was perhaps just as well that Peking Man didn't turn up in Taiwan.

As time passed, and the widow remained in limbo, Janus decided to run the risk of her disapproval by enlisting the F.B.I. to explore the Marine connection. The special agents could find no clues to her from Marine sources. Janus flew out to a reunion of the Camp Holcomb Marine detachment in Dayton, Ohio. The veterans were a mine of information about the bad old days of their surrender to the Japanese, but they were no help to Janus.

One former leatherneck who was most knowledgeable about the Chinese customs guessed:

"Peking Man was long ago dispensed to an ailing Chinese in the form of medicine." If the fossils had been found by a lay prospector for dragon bones in the debris of war, and sold to a drugstore, the trail has come full circle. Some folks who are mystically inclined believe Peking Man resented being disturbed from his grave, and therefore welcomed being turned into medicine, to be swallowed and so vanish forever.

But Dr. Shapiro seems not to accept this solution. That would be giving up. He's not ready to do that. For all anyone knows the boxes may have been hidden in some unlikely place in China and will some day be found.

And Janus has still not given up on the vanished woman, though almost three years have passed since he saw her. Time has tempered his original enthusiasm. He's willing to say:

"This whole thing may be a hoax, but again, I believe she may just have Peking Man."

THE MA & PA MURDERS

For many years after the double murders in Fall River, Massachusetts, little girls all over the country jumped rope to the cheerful rhythm of an anonymous ditty. In four lines it gives a generally accepted solution to the horrendous crime committed on August 4, 1892:

> Lizzie Borden took an axe
> And gave her mother forty wacks
> And when she saw what she had done
> She gave her father forty-one.

Like many present-day singing commercials, the catchy jingle can't stand very close examination. Some of the details are inaccurate. For one thing, the slain woman, Abby Borden, was not Lizzie's mother but her stepmother. For another, the number of blows is greatly exaggerated. A panel of Harvard experts counted fewer than a dozen. And finally, and most important, Lizzie was tried by the Commonwealth of Massachusetts, and was found innocent.

In the case of an unsolved crime, police usually keep all the relevant material in an open file, and the search continues for the murderer. But so far as anyone knows, the police made no other attempt to solve the crime after Lizzie was acquitted. Nor was anyone else ever tried. Of course it isn't unusual for a prosecutor to give up on a case when he has failed to prove his prime suspect guilty. His chances for convincing a jury that he is right the second time when he was wrong the first are negligible.

What makes the Fall River murders different from any other unsolved crimes, is that not long after Lizzie Borden walked out of the courthouse a free woman, self-appointed professional and amateur investigators began trying to reverse the verdict. And they're still trying. Lawyers, playwrights, poets, novelists have not been able to let the dead rest. Lizzie Borden has become a horrifying American legend — a monster who committed the unforgivable crime — murdering her parents.

As recently as the spring of 1975, a nationally broadcast television drama condemned Lizzie again. As the story is retold in every generation, it sometimes ignores her aquittal. Unlike the Fall River police, who arrested Lizzie because she was the most obvious sus-

Lizzie Borden in about 1889.

pect, many contemporary investigators find her guilty by analyzing her unconscious mind. Probings of this sort, even by psychiatrists, are necessarily speculative and, however ingenious, hardly constitute evidence.

It might be that she must be found guilty, for what the case comes down to is if Lizzie didn't kill Abby and Andrew Borden, who did? Well, there was her uncle, John Morse, whom Fall River suspected so strongly at first that he was almost lynched. And Bridget Sullivan, the Borden housemaid. And there was that young stranger, who was seen hanging around the Borden house that bloody day. He was never found, never identified. And what about the numerous enemies Andrew Borden had made on his way from rags to riches.

It was not difficult to dislike and even hate Andrew Borden. Though the well-to-do residents of Fall River regarded him as an uplifting example of what Yankee thrift and shrewdness could accomplish, they had contempt for his miserliness. The son of a fish peddler, he had started out in life as an embalmer, and though he rose to become a bank president, mill owner, and slum landlord, the graveside manner of his beginning remained with him. Tall, gaunt, always dressed in black, he was a caricature of an undertaker.

At the time of his sudden death, Borden had accumulated half-a-million dollars by his ruthless though legal methods of doing business. Among his legion of ill-wishers were the small businessmen he had ruined, the mill hands he relentlessly exploited, the tenants he evicted, and the debtors from whom he exacted usurious interest. There were many in Fall River who were not saddened by his death. And more who regretted that it had not come sooner.

If there were many who might have had reason to hasten Andrew Borden's departure from life, quite the reverse was true about the other victim. Fall River knew she was Andrew's wife, and the stepmother of his two daughters, but it only really became aware of her existence when she was killed. She rarely left her house, had no friends, no interests, no life of her own. The only activity she engaged in, apart from keeping house, was overeating. Today's weight watchers might say that Abby ate so much because she was deprived of any other emotional satisfaction. Whatever the cause, she was grotesque—barely five feet tall, she weighed well over two hundred pounds. She was so ponderous that she would not have been agile enough to avoid the attacker's axe, even if she'd had the opportunity.

Nobody seems to have had much feeling about Abby, one way or another, except Lizzie. Witnesses at the trial testified that Lizzie had come to hate her. They agreed, however, that the relationship between the two had been harmonious, up until almost the end.

Abby was the only mother Lizzie ever knew, her own having died when she was born. Lizzie was two, and her sister Emma twelve, when Andrew made Abby his wife. By the standards of the time, Fall River agreed she was lucky. It was probably the only offer the plain thirty-eight-year-old spinster had ever had. Also, by standards of the time, Andrew Borden had made a sensible deal. Abby cooked his meals, kept his house, and took care of his children. She was careful with his money, never questioned his decisions, knew her place and never budged from it. Not once in thirty years did she give him cause to complain. And there's no reason to doubt she would have gone right on being so "model" a wife if she had been allowed to live to a riper age.

Abby's vegetable existence seemed to have influenced the older girl more than it did the younger. Emma may have patterned herself on Abby because, being ten years older than Lizzie, she mothered her little sister. In any event, when her parents were struck down, Emma was forty-two, evidently not likely to marry. She had few friends and went out almost as infrequently as her stepmother.

Lizzie was different from the other occupants of the somber Borden house on Second Street. Though her ungainly figure and heavy features did not attract gentlemen callers — at thirty-two she was still single — she did not let that inhibit her. She dressed well and had a busy social life. She had many friends who knew her as a warm, kind, and loving person. When there was church welfare work to be done, Lizzie could be counted on to volunteer. It was not only among those of her own station that Lizzie was admired and respected. She was also well thought of on the wrong side of the tracks because of her efforts on behalf of the poor and unfortunate. It was no wonder then, that Fall River was appalled when Lizzie was arrested.

Was Lizzie a Jekyll-Hyde? Behind her open, friendly, selfless exterior was there a secret ogre? It's curious that those whose study of the murders have led them to damn her, affirm that she was exactly what she seemed. That is, until five years before she supposedly took axe in hand.

What happened back then in 1887 was that Andrew Borden made a real estate deal. Before consummating it, he talked the matter over with his first wife's brother, John Morse, whom he trusted for the same virtues he found in himself. Morse was as miserly and rapacious as he. Andrew bought a house, and for reasons of his own, he put the house in Abby's name. He kept the matter a secret.

Though Andrew Borden was not renowned for dealing openly, and nobody knows how many such undercover transactions he'd made during his career, it is alleged that he kept this one secret because he thought his daughters would resent his favoring Abby over them. It's difficult to believe that he intended Abby to be anything but the nominal owner of the property. Nobody knew better than the sisters that Abby was their father's creature. How then could they have decided that Abby was depriving them of their inheritance?

Nevertheless, testimony tells us that both women were furious when the secret came out. Emma swallowed her anger. Lizzie, always the more forthright of the two, blamed Abby for having tricked Andrew into it. Nor did she hide her anger against her Uncle John, for having conspired against her and Emma.

From then on the tepid temperature of the Borden menage turned icy. Lizzie stopped calling Abby mother, and when she mentioned her at all, referred to her stiffly as Mrs. Borden. This change has been taken to mean that murder was brewing.

Except for complaining to her friends about Abby's treachery, and not "mothering her," Lizzie seems to have done nothing to revenge herself for four years. Then the Borden house was robbed. Abby's watch and chain, her few pieces of jewelry, and about a hundred dollars Andrew kept locked in his desk were taken.

Borden reported the crime to the police, but insisted it not be made public. In fact it was not known in Fall River until Lizzie talked about it to a friend, the day before the killings. The robbery took place on one of the rare occasions when the parents were away.

Lizzie's stepmother, Abby Borden.

It resembles the "locked room" mysteries of fiction in which no one can presumably get in or out.

Andrew had locked the doors, as he always did when he went out, closing in his daughters and Bridget. None of the women seemed to have heard anything. Anti-Lizzie researchers conjecture that Lizzie turned thief to pay Abby and Andrew back — that he knew she'd done it and that was why he called off the police.

Immediately preceding the crime there were two events which seem to implicate Lizzie further. One was another of her father's real estate deals, the second a complaint by Abby that she was being poisoned. Just why Andrew should have been looking for additional troubles with his daughters, it's hard to comprehend. But once again he decided to put a piece of property into Abby's name, and let no one in on the secret except John Morse. Once again, Lizzie is supposed to have found out about it, and this time she's supposed to have plotted murder to prevent it.

A pharamacist was to testify that two weeks before the murders, Lizzie tried unsuccessfully to buy prussic acid from him. And the record shows that August 3rd, the day before the murders, Abby went to the doctor to complain she was being poisoned. On the other hand, it also shows that everybody in the household who had eaten the same dinner at noon got sick, including Lizzie. And that

Abby's Dr. Bowen didn't take Abby's poisoning complaint seriously. Fall River was suffering a heat wave, and he diagnosed the cause of her problem as spoiled food.

Surprisingly, Lizzie seems to have disagreed with the doctor. She visited a friend the afternoon of August 3rd and told her she thought someone was trying to poison the family. She chattered on about how the Borden barn had been broken into twice, and about the many enemies her father had made. It was on this occasion that Lizzie revealed for the first time the robbery of the year before. Was this outpouring of revelations part of the murder plan, a clumsy attempt to divert suspicion from herself?

The blistering heat of August 3rd continued through the night and into the morning of August 4th. Except for the weather, everything was as usual in the Borden household. Andrew Borden went downtown sometime after 9 o'clock, and Abby was dusting the dining room when Lizzie appeared. They exchanged polite good mornings. Lizzie was still sick to her stomach and Bridget even sicker. Abby instructed the maid to wash the windows from the outside, and Bridget went to work. Emma had not returned from an overnight visit. Thus, at the beginning of the day, Abby and Lizzie were alone inside the house.

Neighbors observed a young man loitering around the Borden house. While he was not under constant watch, the reports agreed he remained over a period of hours — the time as it turned out when the murders were committed. Those who dismiss the loiterer as a suspect, point out that the murders were done a couple of hours apart. They say it is incredible that he would have entered the house, killed Abby, gone out, waited for Andrew to return and then cut him down. And it is incredible. But for that matter, how credible is it that a young woman of impeccable character and sound mind could have suddenly gone berserk and killed her parents. Yes, there are cases of presumably normal people going crazy. But one notes they inevitably admit their guilt and plead insanity. Not Lizzie. Her insistence on her innocence and her sanity never wavered.

There is some evidence to prove that Andrew Borden waited downtown for his wife to put her signature on the deed. But when he returned home, and Bridget let him in, he didn't ask for his wife. Bridget assumed she was tidying up her bedroom. But Bridget was wrong. For almost two hours, Abby had been lying in her blood in the upstairs guest room.

From Bridget's testimony, we learn that Miss Lizzie came down dressed to go out. She was wearing her hat and, what later seemed suspicious to the police, a heavy, woolen dress — a garment hardly fit for the 110 degree day. She greeted her father, who went upstairs briefly, then joined Lizzie in the sitting room, where he stretched out on a sofa.

Apparently Lizzie changed her mind about going out, for the last Bridget saw of them on her way up to the attic, Lizzie had taken off her hat and was ironing while Andrew was resting.

If we believe Lizzie's account of what happened in that room, darkened against the burning sun, she was the next-to-last person to see Andrew alive. If you don't, she was the last. What is particularly fascinating about this case is that opposite conclusions are built upon the same foundation — the relationship that existed between father and daughter.

It is universally accepted that if Andrew Borden was capable of any act of love or generosity in his seventy years it never came to light. With one exception. He had a soft spot in his heart for the baby of the family. His feeling for her was so strong that it overcame his miserliness. Andrew denied her nothing. Lizzie could waste money on fripperies like dresses, shoes, hats. His extraordinary open-handedness went so far as to allow even such a spendthrift excess as a trip to Europe. For Andrew Borden, to whom money wasn't everything, it was the only thing, no greater proof of love was possible.

And there is no question that Lizzie loved her dour, taciturn father. It may even have had something to do with her not getting married, since in practical, hardheaded Fall River, far less attractive heiresses than Lizzie became brides. But Andrew seems to have been the only man in her life.

Andrew Borden, Lizzie's father.

One concrete sign of the affection between father and daughter was the little gold class ring the girls at Fall River High School got when they graduated. Usually a girl gave the treasured memento to a boy she favored. Lizzie gave hers to her father. And Andrew, who had the undertaker's professional avoidance of ornament, never took Lizzie's ring off his little finger, indeed took it with him into his grave.

You'd think logically that Lizzie's love for her father would make it impossible for anyone to believe she'd harm him. But it is precisely because she loved him so dearly that some psychoanalytical speculations go against her. They take off from the discoveries made by Dr. Sigmund Freud, originator of psychoanalysis, who first explored the workings of the unconscious. Freud pointed out that it was normal for children to love their parents and sometimes to get angry with them and hate them. Moreover, it was characteristic of child-parent relationships that boys tended to become jealous of and competitive with their fathers, and girls have similar attitudes toward their mothers. Because these feelings are socially unacceptable, children soon learn to conceal them. They get buried so deep in the unconscious that young people mature, totally unaware they exist. These repressed emotions are expressed by most people in harmless behavior. But they could provoke an unstable, psychotic person into destructive acts.

Lizzie's accusers say the property deals inflamed her latent jealousy of Abby, and made her furious with her father. But given that Lizzie's mind has been read accurately, one has to ask, jealous and angry enough to murder?

A further attack made on Lizzie's innocence is the theory that when Andrew went upstairs, he discovered his wife's body, then came down and accused Lizzie of murdering her, and Lizzie had to silence him. But is it likely that even so impassive and emotionally granite a man would not have been shaken by the sight of murder and cried out? Would he have accused Lizzie while he was spread out on the couch? That's where Bridget swore she saw him alive when she went up to the attic.

Bridget had rested in her garret for about half an hour when she heard Lizzie scream, "Murder! Help! Father has been murdered!"

What happened during that half hour? Bridget could only tell the court that she ran down the stairs to find Lizzie staring in horror at the battered corpse of her father. Lizzie was to explain that she'd been out in the barn during the thirty minutes, looking for a fishing sinker. When she'd returned she found Andrew killed.

From then on there was hysteria, and a confusion of comings and goings and a welter of conflicting statements among which the jury was to try to sort out the truth. Lizzie sent Bridget for a doctor. A neighbor who responded to Lizzie's screams said Lizzie was distraught and had volunteered that her mother had gone out and she didn't know where she was, but maybe she'd been killed too. Lizzie altered her story when she told it to Doctor Bowen and the police who arrived in quick succession. She said Abby had gone out, but now she added vaguely maybe she had returned.

Dr. Bowen and the police officers examined the body and came to the conclusion that Borden had been killed by a sharp wedge-shaped instrument, like a hatchet. Bowen offered his opinion that the victim had died instantly, any one of the numerous blows would have been enough to kill him. The police were puzzled by Abby's absence, knowing how rarely she went out. Then, horror was added to horror. Bridget, trying to find something to do to blot out the dreadful sight downstairs, went up to dust in the guest room and came on Abby hacked to death.

And the news spread through the town, the inevitable crowd of the morbid, always attracted by murder and disaster, gathered outside the house. It was coming on to noon, and John Morse appeared to take his dinner with the Bordens. It was because Morse was an outsider, who looked like a tramp, and a known conniver in Borden's schemes, that the crowd concluded he was not beyond murder if there was profit in it.

The police had to protect him from the mob. But they held him for questioning and found that he had an alibi for Andrew's

138

murder, though not for Abby's. Since they believed the crimes were the work of one person, they cleared him and he made himself scarce.

At the beginning, the police assumed the murders were the work of an intruder. But when the doctor established that Abby had been killed some two hours before her husband, they couldn't understand where the murderer could possibly have been during the interval.

They looked for the hatchet-shaped murder weapon. Bridget turned up several axe heads from the cellar. Marshall John Fleet, who came to head the inquiry, found one of Bridget's offerings interesting. It was an axe head with a freshly broken-off handle. There was no trace of blood on it, but Fleet reasoned that a steel axe head can be washed clean. But not a wood handle. Perhaps that was why the axe handle had been broken off. The missing handle could not be found. Later on it was conjectured that Lizzie had burned it.

But this early in the proceedings Lizzie was not remotely suspected, even though one of the policemen had gone out to the barn, and had reported to Fleet that it was hotter than the hinges of hell and he couldn't stay in it for more than a few minutes. So how could Lizzie have been there for half an hour? And more peculiar still was that the dust in the barn lay thick and showed no sign of having been disturbed.

However, the next day, when Dr. Bowen

told Fleet about Abby's poisoning, and they learned from druggist Eli Bence that Lizzie without a prescription had tried to buy ten cents worth of prussic acid to clean her fur cape, they turned their attention to her. It began to make sense. For one thing, she would inherit half of Andrew's estate —Emma was never suspected; she was away from home during the murders.

It required courage for the police to suspect one of Fall River's wealthy citizens. They would much rather have picked on Bridget, an Irish immigrant nobody. But Lizzie, to her own peril, made it clear that Bridget couldn't possibly have killed Abby, and had no earthly reason to do away with Andrew.

Lizzie was the most promising candidate, in fact, the only lead the authorities had, and they devoted themselves exclusively to nailing her. Since the axe had spilled so much blood, it stood to reason that the killer's clothes would bear the stains of the crime. They searched the house for a blood-stained garment. They found none. A second, more thorough, search also failed. Though it must certainly have been clear to Lizzie that she was the only suspect, she did not object when the police asked her, politely of course, for her shoes, stockings, undergarments, and wool dress. These, as well as the axe head were sent to the Harvard medical experts for microscopic examination.

On the advice of the family lawyer, Andrew J. Jennings, the sisters offered a $5,000 reward for the murderer. No one appeared with any information. The local newspapers, without mentioning Lizzie by name, implied she was the logical suspect. Stories quoted the police theory that the criminal was a woman. And when the public read that Andrew Borden had died without leaving a will, so that Lizzie and Emma would inherit a vast sum of money, well, there was a sufficient motive for murder.

Several thousand uninvited citizens gathered at the cemetery for the final rites. But those who had come to look at the conscience-stricken face of guilt were disappointed. Lizzie was composed, impassive, pale in her weeds, showing nothing but the emotional restraint proper to native New England mourners. It could have been any funeral except that just as the coffins were about to be lowered into the grave, the police halted the service. The internment would be indefinitely delayed — an autopsy had been ordered. This dramatic turn of events made the whole occasion worthwhile for the home folks who now had something to talk about.

During the week after the murders, there was a constant stream of visitors to the Borden house. Mostly they were Lizzie's friends, acquaintances, good-works associates. They came to offer their condolences, along with the ritual calf's foot jellies, cakes, and other homemade dainties. In effect they were rallying round Lizzie, acting, so to speak, as character witnesses in her defense against the hints and innuendos of the press.

However, their good intentions were to be used against Lizzie, for when it was announced that the inquest into the murders was to be held in private, the papers suggested that it was a cover-up by Lizzie's influential and rich peers.

Just how much effect this stirring up of sentiment would have had on the outcome of the inquest if Lizzie had been a good witness in her own behalf is difficult to say. The fact is that, subjected to intensive questioning, Lizzie gave confusing and contradictory answers. Yes, she knew Abby had gone out. No, she only thought so. She had been in the barn. No, in the hayloft. She had found the sinker. She hadn't found it. She was out of the house for twenty minutes at least. She wasn't sure how long. And so on.

Unquestionably, Lizzie's performance on the stand did not prove her innocence. This, in the opinion of her defenders, is what she had been required to do. There was still no hard evidence against her. One could reasonably expect that the coroner's finding would have been "Murder by person and persons as yet unknown." And further investigation by the police would have been ordered. A decision of this sort would not have cleared Lizzie, but it might have led the police to at least consider other possible suspects, however remote. They never did, for the inquest charged Lizzie with suspicion of murdering her parents and remanded her to prison, pending arraignment and pre-trial legal proceedings.

What a humdinger of a story it made for the newspapers! Not only the most horrendous of crimes, but the accused is a woman, and an heiress. And throw in that she is a pillar of the church, and add that she is active in worthy causes; well, reporters from all over the country took off for Fall River.

One of them came up with a scoop during the nine months Lizzie was in prison. He wormed out of prison matron Regan a conversation she claimed to have overheard between Lizzie and Emma. On one of Emma's daily visits the sisters had got into an argument. According to Mrs. Regan, Lizzie screamed at Emma, "You are giving me away!" Mrs. Regan was not called by the State to swear to this statement until the trial.

The testimony of druggist Eli Bence strongly influenced the outcome of the arraignment. His straightforward account of Lizzie's vain attempt to buy poison added an additional horrifying dimension to Lizzie's character. The implications were obvious. She must have or may have found a less ethical pharmacist whom she could persuade to sell her the ten cents worth of prussic acid. And because the police had not been able to find any such vendor, there was a fallback assumption that she probably got it somehow, and sprinkled Abby's food with it. Once you accept these assumptions, you can answer the question: "How come everybody who ate the same dinner the day before the murders got sick?" That was probably a cunning attempt by the accused to shield herself. Abby got the lethal dose, the others only enough to make it seem like summer complaint.

This structure lacked only the connecting mortar of fact. But legends need more than prosaic reality to build on. We create them out of our brightest dreams and darkest fears. And built high upon Bence's account was the terrifying image of a daughter who killed her parents, not in a frenzy of uncontrollable rage — but with cold, calculated, premeditated intent.

When the representatives of the Harvard medicos took the stand they reported their laboratory tests had revealed no traces of blood on the axe head, nor on Lizzie's shoes, stockings, wool dress, or any other clothing except for a red speck on an underskirt. Under oath, Lizzie attributed it to a flea — a not uncommon inhabitant of even the most splendid Fall River homes of the day.

Jennings, Lizzie's lawyer, placed great emphasis on the gory nature of the crime. The ferocity of the attack must have splashed the killer's clothes with blood. He stressed that despite the most thorough search by the police — on two separate occasions — no stained garment of any kind has been found. Without such evidence, he contended, Lizzie could not be linked to the crime. Though his argument weighed in his client's favor, the court found that there was enough reason to hold Lizzie for the grand jury, and she was sent back to prison.

Public opinion, at best unstable, now began to tilt toward Lizzie. The papers found that many people believed she was being hounded and persecuted — was being made the scapegoat of police failure to find the real murderer. This change in attitude resulted in considerable part from the willingness of prominent individuals and groups to insist publicly on her innocence.

Her pastor proclaimed his faith in Lizzie; her associates in the women's auxiliary of the Y.M.C.A. prayed for her; the Women's Christian Temperance Union backed her; suffragists and members of the women's rights movement spoke and protested in her behalf. Lizzie was becoming a controversial cause.

The arguments, pro and con, heated up when the Grand Jury convened to decide whether to indict her. It was then for the first time that Alice Russell, Emma's friend, was called to testify by the prosecution. Miss Russell related what had occurred while she was visiting the sisters on Sunday morning, three days after the murder. Emma and she were chatting in the kitchen when Lizzie appeared with a dress, splotched with brown smears, that she proceeded to tear into shreds and burn in the kitchen stove. The witness said Lizzie had explained the stains were brown paint which she couldn't get off and which had made the dress useless.

The record did note that the burning of the dress took place a day after the police for the second time had searched in vain for a blood-stained garment. All that seems to have meant to the jurymen was that Lizzie had outsmarted the police. But why, having so successfully hidden this damning evidence, she should have burned it in front of a witness, is a hard-to-answer question. Whether they asked it of themselves is not known. But they considered the evidence offered by witnesses sufficiently incriminating to conclude that Lizzie Borden must stand trial for murder.

The case of The People vs. Lizzie Borden began nine months after she was arrested. Pale from her long prison confinement, she stood before the three justices and the jury in the New Bedford courthouse to listen to the charge against her. Once again, she answered the question "How do you plead?" with a firm "Not guilty."

Appearing as the principal counsel for the defense was George Robinson, a renowned trial lawyer from Boston. The prosecution was represented by a team noted for its record of convictions, headed by Hosea Knowlton. In terms of skill and ability oppos-

The Borden house, where the famous murders took place.

ing counsel were well matched. The prosecutors could be confident, on the basis of testimony given at the previous hearings, that they had evidence enough to condemn her.

But they ran into a snag at the outset when they tried to introduce the fumbling, contradictory statements the defendant had made at the inquest. Defense counsel cited the law when he objected, pointing out that Lizzie had been under arrest and not been informed of her right not to testify. The objection was sustained by the court.

Three doctors from Harvard, put on the stand in turn by the prosecution, testified that even the deepest of the blows that mutilated the victims could have been made by a woman. But the State's claim that the axe head was the murder weapon became questionable when cross-examination elicited from the experts that not all of the cuts could have been made by the axe.

The prosecution's case was further shaken when Lizzie's counsel cross-questioned the doctor about the blood spot found on her underskirt. The Harvard laboratory test had disclosed it was not human blood; this helped substantiate Lizzie's flea explanation. The court upheld the defense objection to druggist Bence's poison story on the ground that no connection had been proved between that and the murders. After ten days, having made substantially the same case that had brought

Lizzie to trial, the prosecution rested.

A basic premise for the defense was that the police, unable to find the real criminal, were trying to frame Lizzie. Robinson undermined the credibility of the police witness who testified he'd gone into the barn and had found the dust undisturbed, by producing two surprise witnesses. They were teenagers, Tom Barlow and Everett Brown.

If the jury believed the policeman, then Lizzie was lying when she said she'd been in the barn while her father was murdered. But when they heard the boys' story, they must have had their doubts. These Fall River equivalents of Tom Sawyer and Huck Finn related that they visited the scene of the crime shortly after the news broke, to find the murderer. Unable to gain entrance to the house, they had gone into the barn where they'd searched high and low for clues. The prosecution did its best to discredit the youngsters who must have left obvious signs of their presence. But it couldn't budge them.

Seeking support for the frame-up theory, the defense called an itinerant ice cream vendor to the stand. This witness, an immigrant, testified in his broken English that he'd seen Lizzie go out to the barn as he was passing the house. The prosecution poked fun at his accent, got big laughs by bewildering him with rapid-fire questions, thus rendering his testimony practically worthless.

Critical to the outcome of the trial was the

issue of the stained dress Lizzie had burned. Robinson approached this matter by first trying to establish that, contrary to the thrifty Fall River custom of keeping useless clothing in a rag bag, Lizzie discarded things she wasn't going to wear again. When the prosecution objection that this was irrelevant was sustained, Emma was called as a defense witness.

Of course, her statement was discounted in advance. Nobody expected her to testify against Lizzie. But she went further. She swore she had suggested to Lizzie that the old, paint-stained dress be burned. And she stuck to her story.

In his summation Robinson reviewed the totally circumstantial nature of the case against Lizzie. He reminded the members of the jury that to find Lizzie guilty they must agree with the prosecution that her motive for murder was a real estate dispute. They must not reasonably doubt that a woman of blameless character, a church worker, was suddenly transformed into a arch-fiend because her father had transferred a piece of property to her mother — a piece of property worth only $1,500.

They must further believe that the axe head which they had heard an acknowledged expert testify was identical with countless others made in the same factory, was the murder weapon — an assertion made by the prosecution, entirely without proof.

And finally, to find the defendant guilty they must convince themselves that she was, as the state claimed, at once a cunning criminal and a blundering idiot. Could they believe with Mr. Knowlton, that the same person who was shrewd enough to conceal the incriminating evidence of the bloody dress from the police was also stupid enough to burn it in the presence of witnesses *while policemen were around and about the house*?

When Knowlton's turn came to sum up, he seemed to be advocating the unpopular feminist position of the '90's as he told the all-male jury, "Women are not better and no worse than we are." His purpose of course was to counter the Victorian belief that a woman — the defendant specifically — was a delicate, fragile being, incapable of violence. Pursuing his theme, he cited instances of murders committed by women of impeccable reputation, some even church workers. He referred back to the medical testimony that the death blows could have been committed by a woman. And who else but this woman had the opportunity and the motive?

What was the motive? "Malice against Mrs. Borden inspired the assassin!" Abby Borden had no enemies but Lizzie. Why was Andrew Borden hacked to death? The jury should bear in mind that the Lizzie Borden who came down from the guest room in which she had left her stepmother dead was not Andrew Borden's loving daughter, but a murderess. It was in fear of retribution that she took the axe to him.

Why had Lizzie burned the blood-stained dress? Because she had no alternative. Because she knew that the police would search for it again, and it was safer to get rid of it at all costs, rather than run the risk of having this incontrovertible evidence found. As Knowlton concluded there was a stir in the courtroom while the justices conferred. The spectators argued in whispers about the outcome. Many wondered what the jury would make of Lizzie's not taking the stand in her own defense? Of course it was her constitutional right, but then wouldn't that be construed as an admission of guilt?

Silence fell as the chief judge began to speak. Before he instructed the jury, he said, he wanted to give the defendant an opportunity to speak. Lizzie rose slowly. "I am innocent," she said. That was all.

In his charge to the jury, the judge pointed out that "by seeking only the truth, you will lift this case above the range of passion and excited feeling, into the clear atmosphere of reason and law...."

The jury was out for only an hour. When they returned having reached the legally required unanimous decision, Lizzie was told to stand to receive their judgment. The impassive composure she had maintained during her long ordeal was shattered by the foreman's "Not guilty." Lizzie broke into tears. The spectators cheered and applauded the verdict. The next day's newspapers celebrated the "victory of justice."

The sisters returned to Fall River where they bought an elaborate house which they lived in together for twelve years. Then Emma moved out because it seemed she felt that Lizzie and she should lead a retired life of mourning. Lizzie would have none of that. She gave parties, and took up her active social life.

Through the years she never made any attempt to seclude herself, as many in Fall River thought would be more proper for a person tried for murder. Lizzie was among the first in town to buy an automobile, in which she took daily drives. Fall River noted disapprovingly that she was always going to the theater in Boston and New York. In 1923, the sisters got into a dispute about some real estate. It resulted in a lawsuit which brought the Bordens back into the newspapers again. Emma dropped the case and retired into obscurity in New Hampshire. Thirty-five years after her acquittal, Lizzie Borden, aged 67, died of natural causes in Fall River hospital. Ten days later, Emma Borden died. The sisters lie in Fall River cemetery, in the family plot, beside their mother, father, and stepmother. Lizzie continued her good works after her death, leaving her money to an animal refuge.

Lizzie has not been allowed to rest in

peace. The hope expressed in the court's charge to the jury has not been fulfilled. The case has not been lifted "above passion and excited feeling, into the clear atmosphere of reason and law." It probably will never be.